# *Mum to Mum*

Also by Coleen Nolan

*Upfront and Personal*

COLEEN NOLAN

# Mum to Mum

Happy Memories and Honest
Advice from a Real Mum

SIDGWICK & JACKSON

First published 2010 by Sidgwick & Jackson
an imprint of Pan Macmillan, a division of Macmillan Publishers Limited
Pan Macmillan, 20 New Wharf Road, London N1 9RR
Basingstoke and Oxford
Associated companies throughout the world
www.panmacmillan.com

ISBN 978-0-283-07107-2 HB
ISBN 978-0-283-07122-5 TPB



Illustrations by Jacky Fleming



1 3 5 7 9 8 6 4 2

A CIP catalogue record for this book is available from
the British Library.

Printed in UK by CPI Mackays, Chatham ME5 8TD

*To my mum, my true inspiration, who taught me so much and who I miss every day*

## DISCLAIMER

This book is intended as an anecdotal and informal advice book for mums out there trying to cope with the trials and tribulations of bringing up a young family, based on the author's own life and experience. It is important to bear in mind that you should not consider the author an expert or professional in any given field, or qualified to give professional advice on legal, medical or financial issues.

The diet suggestions in Chapter Four are meant as general advice on healthy eating and are not intended as a substitute for any diet that you may have been prescribed by your doctor. Please consult your doctor before following this diet plan.

Mention of specific companies, organizations or authorities in this book does not imply endorsement of the publisher, nor does mention of specific companies, organizations or authorities in the book imply that they endorse the book. Addresses, websites and telephone numbers given in this book were correct at the time of going to press.

Accordingly neither the publisher nor the author is liable for any direct or indirect loss or injury sustained from your use of any of the information contained in the book or available from companies, organizations or authorities referred to in it.

Every effort has been made to contact copyright holders of the photographs reproduced in this book. If any have been inadvertently overlooked the publishers will be pleased to make restitution at the earliest opportunity.

# Contents

# *Introduction*

When I became a mum, what helped me more than anything else was the support and advice I got from other mums. I learnt to be a better parent by listening to my own mother, my sisters and my friends who'd all had children before me. When I had my first child, Shane Junior, I honestly don't know how I'd have got through that first year without those women. If Shane so much as yawned in a funny way, I'd be on the phone to one of them asking if it was 'normal'.

I could relate to their advice because it came from real experiences and had been handed down through the years from mum to mum. Listening to their stories was so reassuring because it helped me realize I wasn't the only mum in the world to come up against all these worries and problems – and I certainly wouldn't be the last.

So, five years ago, when I started writing my parenting column for the *Daily Mirror*, that's the kind of advice I wanted to pass on to readers – real advice for real mums. I didn't want to preach or tell women what they 'should' be doing to bring up their kids, just to share all the brilliant tips I'd picked up from the mums I'd met and what I'd learnt from my own experiences, too.

There's no doubt that being a mum is the most rewarding thing you'll ever do in life, but it can be tough and even scary at times. You need a never-ending supply of patience, particularly as they grow older, noisier and naughtier! You have to realize that sometimes you will make mistakes with your children, because nobody's perfect. Loving them unconditionally and doing the absolute best you can for them is all that any mum can do.

You also have to accept that you'll worry – a lot! When you become a mum, the phrase 'I promise to worry about you constantly till the day I die' ought to be written into the terms and conditions. You'll never stop worrying about your kids, so don't fight it. My tip is to learn to live with it.

It also helps to know that often there is no 'right way' to handle certain situations. Being a mum is a lot about trial and error. If I've learnt one thing during my twenty-one years as a parent, it's that all kids are different and what works for one doesn't necessarily work for the other. It's about tackling each situation as it arises and finding a solution that works for you.

The other thing that's vital is a bloody good sense of humour. I've turned up for jobs with head lice that my kids have given me.

Scratching your head every five minutes on live TV isn't a winning look, trust me. I lost count of the times I got all dressed up when the children were babies only for one of them to throw up over the shoulder of my posh evening frock. When you have kids, you never know what life is going to fling at you next, but it's a lot easier if you can find the funny side of every situation. If you can take a couple of minutes every day to laugh at whatever ridiculous predicament you find yourself in, then it doesn't seem so bad.

I've had to negotiate quite a few difficult situations in my time. When my sons, Shane Junior and Jake, were little I had to support them while I was divorcing their dad, Shane Richie. I've struggled to lose my baby weight and I've had to rebuild my life as a single mum. Then when I met my husband, Ray Fensome, and we had our daughter, Ciara, who's now eight, we had two years of hell while we all got used to living together as a new family. But we got through it.

And recently I realized something wonderful – I've actually done a pretty good job as a mum. It's not that I ever thought I was a bad mum, it's just that you hardly ever get told what a great mum you are, least of all by the kids, who are usually too concerned with their lift home or their clean football kit or what they're having for tea that night to turn round and say, 'Thanks, Mum! I love you.'

But in March 2009, when I was competing in *Dancing on Ice*, my sons, Shane Junior, who's now twenty-one and Jake, who's seventeen, did an interview with the *Daily Mirror*, talking about what it was like to have me as their mum and how grateful they were that we had such a close relationship.

I was totally blown away by it. What moved me the most was to hear them say they never felt they'd suffered when I was divorcing their dad because I'd always explained things to them in a way they could understand and had reassured them we'd still love them as much no matter what happened. It meant so much to me because when my marriage to Shane ended the thing that upset me most was this awful feeling I'd failed my children. To hear how much the boys appreciated everything I'd done for them was worth every tear and every sleepless night.

You're going to be hearing quite a bit about my family in this book, so now is probably as good a time as any to introduce them.

First of all there's my eldest son, Shane Junior. When he was a toddler he used to have major temper tantrums that lasted for two hours a day, but he's grown into such a laid-back adult. He's non-confrontational, just like me. And he's very much a leader – even at school he was never bothered about wearing the same trainers as everyone else, he'd just go his own way. He did two years as a Pontin's Blue Coat and I'll never forget going to see him in a show for the first time. He had this amazing voice and was dancing and lifting girls over his head! I just looked at Ray and said, 'Where the hell did all that come from?' I was dead proud of him.

Jake is more volatile than Shane and he's very passionate about everything he does. Jake didn't grow out of his temper – he still sees red. He wants to be an actor and he's great at singing and dancing. He also has a really sensitive side and cares a lot about people. He's protective of me and very loyal. When I'm old, Jake will be the one who'll come to visit me and bring me food parcels.

And Ciara, I have to say, is just a doll. She's never had a tantrum and she bypassed the Terrible Twos completely. She's a really chilled-out kid and very kind. I don't think I've ever had to raise my voice to her. I was thirty-six when I had her and it was a very different experience to having the boys in my early twenties. I was a much more relaxed parent in my thirties and I think that rubbed off on her. I'm convinced she's storing up all her bad behaviour for her teens when those hormones kick in, so I'm preparing myself.

Then, last but not least, there's my husband Ray, who I met in a bar in Blackpool in 2000. He restored my faith in men and gave me a second chance at love and marriage. He loves Shane and Jake as much as he loves Ciara and they've grown to love and respect him, too. He's a much stricter parent than I am, which is good because I'm pretty soft, so we balance each other out. We make a good team.

I've loved putting together this book of family stories and Q&As from my *Daily Mirror* parenting column 'Mum to Mum', and it's brought back loads of wonderful memories from when

Shane and Jake were little. It's also made me realize just how quickly those childhood years go by – my boys have grown-up and left home now. My advice to all mums is to make sure you stop now and again to make the most of the time with your children when they're young.

More than anything, writing this book has made me certain of one thing – even when your kids are driving you up the wall, being a mum is still the best job in the world. And don't let anyone tell you any different.

ONE

# Their First Year

# Oh, Baby, You've Done It Now!

I'll never forget walking out of the hospital after having Shane Junior. I had this tiny helpless baby in my arms and I just thought, 'God, now it really is down to me.' It was the most exciting moment of my life, but also the most terrifying.

With your first child, you really have no idea – every day something new happens that you have to deal with. You feel you're expected to know instinctively what to do because you're now a mum, but there are plenty of times when you think, 'I haven't got a clue.' And that's OK. You're not a bad parent, you're a first-time parent. Never be ashamed to ask for help from family and friends. I must have spent the first six months of Shane's life on the phone to my mum bombarding her with questions. The important thing is that you don't feel you're on your own.

I remember once when Shane was only a few weeks old, he started crying at nine o'clock in the morning and at seven o'clock that night, he was still crying. I'd tried everything – winding him, feeding him, changing him. I began to get angry because I was so tired and the incessant crying was driving me crazy. I ended up screaming, 'I don't know what you want!' then burst into tears because I'd shouted at my baby. I called a friend who lived round the corner and he came over. He told me to get a cup of tea and sit down, and that he'd take care of Shane for a bit. That's all I needed – someone who could be there for an hour and deal with it. It didn't mean I couldn't cope or that I was a terrible mum, I just needed a break.

Probably the hardest thing is finding a routine after you've brought your new baby home. I remember thinking, 'What the hell do I do with Shane when I want to have a shower?' He ended up going everywhere with me in his car seat, including the toilet! But gradually, you do get into a routine and become more relaxed. You realize that very little babies can't move, so if they're in a safe place it won't harm them if they cry for a bit while you're having a wee!

Of course when your second and third babies come along, you're much more easy-going. When the first one cries, you're at their side in a flash, but when the others come along, God love them, you're like, 'Ah, shut up, I'll get to you in a minute!' I was a much more relaxed parent by the time Ciara came along and I enjoyed it more, too. Having already had two children I knew how quickly the time goes – they don't stay babies for long. So my advice is to relish every moment.

Nothing beats the excitement of seeing your baby reach all those milestones in their first year. The first smile they give you when they're only a few weeks old is just magical. Every new stage is a thrill – the first time they sit up on their own, their first steps, their first words. I loved it when Shane Junior giggled for the first time. He was about three months old and suddenly started chuckling hysterically. We were in raptures watching him.

There's no doubt that during those first few months there will be times when you feel overwhelmed by tiredness, but you realize when you look back that they are the best days of your life.

It's easy to point out all the stressful bits, but it's impossible to remember all the good times because there are just too many of them. Even if I'd had the day from hell with my kids when they were babies, I'd get them all bathed and snuggly in a little babygro, they'd fall asleep and everything just melted away. I'd look at them in awe and think, 'This is the best thing I've ever done.' It's fabulous.

# How Soon Should I Get Into a Routine With my New Baby?

**I'm due to have my first baby soon and want to know if I should start a routine the first day I bring her home from hospital or if I should let her settle first. Have you any tips?**

Hmmm, this is a hotly debated topic. Some parenting experts believe in a strict clock-driven schedule for your baby when it comes to resting, playing and feeding from when they're just a few days old. Others believe in a much more relaxed approach where you kind of leave it to the baby to dictate the routine.

I think you have to get the baby into *your* routine and way of life, and rely on gut instinct and common sense when it comes to what your baby needs and when. As long as your baby is content, and feeding and sleeping well, that's the main thing. It has to be a routine that works for you.

When I had Shane Junior people used to tell me to keep him to a strict schedule during the day so he wouldn't get up till six in the morning, but I couldn't think of anything worse than getting up that early because I'm a night person. So I ended up giving all my babies a feed around 11 p.m., then they'd sleep till eight or nine o'clock, which was better for me.

Don't worry if your little one isn't a textbook baby who wakes up every four hours for a feed. Shane Junior would have slept for fifteen hours flat if I'd let him! Jake and Ciara, on the other hand, would wake regularly for feeds. However, when Shane got to about one, he decided he'd had enough of sleeping and I used to sit up with him watching bad movies until four or five in the morning!

# The Big Sleep: Sweet Dreams for Them (and for You!)

One of the subjects I get the most letters about at the *Daily Mirror* is sleep – or more precisely, the lack of it.

The first year of being a new parent is hard. No one can describe the tiredness you feel from all the nights of broken sleep. Friends try to warn you, but you just can't imagine it. I lost count of the number of people who told me to get plenty of sleep while I was pregnant because once the baby was born I'd never sleep again. I remember thinking, 'How ridiculous. How can something so small create that much havoc?' I didn't believe them. Then I had Shane Junior and felt like I had jet-lag every day. But after having three kids, I have learnt a thing or two about how to get your baby into a routine at night and boost your chances of a good sleep:

- **Make sure they snooze during the day.** Naps in the morning and early afternoon prevent them becoming over tired and cranky at bedtime – just make sure your baby doesn't sleep too late in the afternoon or they won't go down at night. Plenty of fresh air and activity during the day will also help them sleep better in the evening.

- **Have a wind-down routine before bed – and stick to it.** No matter what else is going on in your house, make sure nothing interrupts the calming evening wind-down of bath time, babygro, a bottle, a story and then bed. This helps your baby recognize it's time for sleep.
- **Put them down and leave.** Don't allow your baby to fall asleep with you there or while you're feeding. Put them in their cot awake and let them fall asleep by themselves. You might have to brace yourself for some crying, but they will settle eventually and, if you persevere, they will get into a routine. While you shouldn't leave young babies to cry for long, don't be scared to let older ones cry for a bit – they won't be scarred by it! Do you remember anything from when you were a few months old?
- **Don't pick them up.** It's normal for babies to wake up during the night and cry, but, when they do, resist the urge to pick them up. Go to them and maybe pat their tummy or stroke their head to comfort them, then leave again.
- **Sleep when they sleep.** If your baby goes down for a nap during the day, use the opportunity to have a sleep yourself. Forget the cleaning, the ironing, the mountain of washing – it can all wait. I used to have a snooze on the sofa when Ciara slept. And don't feel guilty – if you're exhausted, the best thing you can do for you and your baby is to recharge your batteries. If you can't sleep, do something else to relax for an hour: put your feet up and watch a bit of daytime telly, have

a bubble bath or read your favourite mag – anything that helps you switch off.

### *Safe Sleeping Rules*

Every new mum worries that something will happen to their baby if they're not staring at them 24/7. It's natural to feel anxious, particularly if you're a first-time parent. I was constantly checking on Shane Junior.

The Department of Health has guidelines to help prevent cot death (sometimes known as sudden infant death syndrome or SIDS). Thankfully, this is rare and you mustn't let worrying about it stop you enjoying those first months with your baby. Follow these rules when you put your baby down – it should help them get a better night's sleep, too:

- Put your baby on their back to sleep. It's recommended your baby should sleep in a cot in a room with you for the first six months.
- Don't let your baby get too hot. Keep their head uncovered and never put them down on an electric blanket or with a hot-water bottle. Make sure their cot isn't next to a heater or in direct sunshine.
- Place them in the 'feet to foot' position (with their feet at the foot of the cot) to prevent them slipping under the bedclothes, and tuck the blanket in at shoulder height.

- Don't smoke in pregnancy or let anyone smoke in the same room as you or your baby.
- Don't share a bed with your baby if you've been drinking alcohol, taking drugs or are a smoker.
- Never sleep with your baby on a sofa or armchair.
- For more information visit www.fsid.org.uk.

## What Should I Do When She Rolls Over at Night?

**My daughter keeps rolling over on to her front when asleep in her cot. Should I roll her back over or just leave her?**

Some people suggest swaddling babies to prevent them rolling on to their tummies, but in the summer months be careful not to make your daughter too hot. You can buy easy swaddling wraps with self-fastening tabs for a snug fit – try www.bloomingmarvellous.co.uk.

As babies get older, though, they will naturally start rolling over on to their tummies. If you find your baby sleeping on her front before she's five or six months old, gently turn her over. But no one can be expected to check for this constantly through the night. At five to six months, the risk of cot death falls rapidly. At this age it's normal for babies to roll over and they shouldn't be prevented from doing so, but still put her on her back to sleep.

## She Prefers Our Bed to Her Own

**My one-year-old caught a cold a few weeks ago. Because she was crying so much, I moved her into my bed so I could look after her. She's now better and I've tried to move her back to her cot, but she won't settle. What can I do?**

This is always a tricky one and you feel torn as a mum because you want to protect them. But you have to be strong! I've been in the same situation and can understand why you moved her into your bed. It's an instinctive thing to do as a mum – if your child is ill, you want them to be close to you. The trouble is, she feels settled there even though she's better. What you have to do now is break the habit. The main tip here is perseverance. She will settle eventually, but she won't if she realizes that every time she cries she'll get taken into Mummy's bed.

From now on, when she cries, go in and perhaps even stroke her a little, but don't pick her up or she'll know that by crying she'll get what she wants. I used to hear the kids crying and I'd go in and gently say 'Shush' then go back to bed. Then the next time I'd go in and say nothing, but they knew I was there and felt reassured.

Give it a few days and she will gradually get used to the changes. It's hard, but you have to be tough about it.

## What Will Ease His Teething Pain?

**My five-month-old has just started teething and is screaming his head off. He's dribbling a lot and his cheeks are really red. What can I do to ease his pain?**

Thank God for Calpol, that's all I can say! I couldn't have managed without it.

Obviously you have to follow the medicine's instructions very carefully and you can't rely on it every day, but at times like these it's a godsend. There are also Bonjela products and gel rings you can put in the fridge and give to a baby to bite on to numb the pain. Bickiepegs teething biscuits, which they can chew on, are also good (www.bickiepegs.co.uk). The relief is usually only temporary, though, and in all honesty there's not much you can do until the tooth breaks through and their pain eases. It's usually the first one that causes the most problems.

Once that comes through it softens the gum for the others and the process is easier. Make sure you give him lots of cuddles and plenty of reassurance that everything is OK.

It'd be great if someone could invent a complete cure because it's horrible seeing your child in pain, but once the tooth breaks through it's amazing how quickly it stops hurting.

## Streamline Your Baby Kit

When you become a mum for the first time, you'll be astounded (and confused) by the number of products and gadgets that you apparently 'absolutely must have'. Well, let me let you into a secret – you don't need most of these things. One mum told me she'd bought a pump designed to extract snot when her baby had a cold. Forget it! Babies survived before snot pumps were invented. And believe me, when you have a buggy to manoeuvre, a toddler in tow and a handbag full of your own useless stuff, the last thing you want to do is lug around a bag full of baby things that weigh a ton. Trust me, here's all you need:

- Muslins – lightweight and perfect for feeding and burping. Also good for dealing with snot and poo.

- Bottles and formula if you're not breastfeeding or solid food if your baby's older.
- Calpol – this cure-all helps with everything from teething and colds to sickness. I couldn't have managed without it.
- Nappies.
- A couple of small plastic bags for dirty clothes and nappies.
- Baby wipes.
- A dummy.
- A couple of small toys.
- Travel-sized products – Johnson's and Avent both do sets with travel-sized versions of everyday baby products.

## A Word About Yummy-Mummy Competition

We've all seen those supermums at the school gates or at the park looking perfectly groomed on four hours' sleep with their all-singing, all-dancing top-of-the-range buggies that do everything except wipe the baby's bum, not to mention their posh changing bags and designer baby slings. It doesn't half make you feel inadequate, eh?

If you can manage it, my advice to all new mums is to avoid yummy-mummy competition from day one, otherwise it can become a very pricey pastime! Buying a buggy has become like choosing a new car – the trouble is, just like cars, there's always a better one that comes along a few months later.

It's understandable that you want the best of everything for your first child and it has to be brand spanking new. I was like that when I had Shane Junior and turned down loads of offers of hand-me-down cots and buggies. By the time Jake came along, I was well over that – as long as stuff worked, I was happy. I used loads of Shane's old baby equipment and clothes and when Jake needed a new pram, I picked one up from a second-hand shop. When you've had one baby you realize how quickly they grow out of things, so bankrupting yourself to buy the latest gear just isn't worth it. What's more, vintage stuff is trendy again!

These days, you can pick up great quality equipment online from sites such as eBay that'll cost you a fraction of the price of buying it new. The National Childbirth Trust (NCT) also runs nearly new sales, selling everything from prams and toys to changing mats and clothes. To find a sale in your area, log on to www.nct.org.uk.

Just think, with the money you save you can treat yourself to a new haircut or a relaxing facial – just before you next meet the local yummy mummies for a coffee. You deserve it!

# Help, My Baby's a Thumb Sucker!

**My eight-month-old son likes to suck his thumb but I've heard a dummy might be a better option. Should I get him to start using a dummy or is it a bad habit to get into?**

I would give him a dummy. I ended up giving all my kids dummies because I can't bear to see older children sucking their thumbs. Thumb-sucking is a much harder habit to break. You can give them a dummy up to a certain age, then just throw it away. You'll have a few days of hell, but they'll get used to it and they'll be fine. On the other hand, what can you do about a thumb? You can't get rid of that! I've seen kids of thirteen who are still sucking their thumbs. It's a big problem. When my niece was seven she was constantly sucking her thumb and it was a nightmare for my sister to get her to stop.

If I were you, I'd introduce your son to a dummy now. It's possible he may find it harder now he's taken to his thumb, but he is still only eight months old so you can probably persuade him. He obviously just wants a comforter. If you can get him to take to a dummy, I think you'll be grateful in the long term – it's just so much easier when you want him to stop. Put it this way, I've never seen a child walking to school with a dummy, but I've seen lots with their thumbs in their mouths!

# Breastfeeding: The Big Debate

## *Am I a Bad Mum If I Can't Do It?*

At the risk of being shot down in flames, I'm going to hold my hands up and admit that I didn't breastfeed either of my sons, even with all the pressure there was to do it. It just wasn't for me. When Ciara came along, I thought she'd probably be my last baby and I was determined to breastfeed her, and Ray wanted me to do it, too. I spent about six weeks trying, but it just didn't work for me – Ciara wasn't getting enough milk and I got mastitis. Even if my arm brushed my breast, the pain was unbelievable. Ray came down one night when I was feeding Ciara. I was sobbing, and he said, 'This is ridiculous.' After that we put her on the bottle and it was a huge relief. I remember thinking, 'Never again!'

Having said that, if you can breastfeed and you want to do it, I think it's absolutely the best start you can give your baby; the milk provides all the nutrition babies need for the first six months. Some health experts also believe that breastfed babies are at a lower risk of conditions such as eczema, asthma and gastroenteritis. And it's convenient – there's no sterilizing of bottles, it's the right temperature – and it's free. It also helps some women lose their baby weight after the birth. My sister Bernie breastfed for eight months and she loved it.

What I don't believe in, though, is giving mums who don't or can't breastfeed a hard time. It's difficult enough having a new baby and, if you're being made to feel like a failure because you've given up on breastfeeding, it only adds to the pressure. So don't beat yourself up if you can't do it. At the end of the day, you have to decide what's right for you, your baby and your family unit.

If you want help with breastfeeding, speak to your doctor or health visitor. There's some good information online – try www.nct.org.uk or call the NCT helpline on 0300 3300 771.

## Ways to Make Breastfeeding Easier

**Wear a bra.** You need this to support your breasts from underneath, but avoid underwired styles as these have been linked to plugged milk ducts and mastitis.

**Make sure you're in a comfortable position.** Support your back and arms with pillows, and put a pillow or cushion on your lap to raise your baby if you need to.

**Get off to a good start.** Gently stroke your baby's cheek nearest your breast and they should turn automatically to start feeding. Make sure you get the nipple well inside the mouth to ensure they're feeding properly – it'll help prevent sore nipples, too!

**Talk to them.** Chat softly to boost feelings of contentment and calm, and keep feeding as long as your baby shows interest. Gently take your baby off the breast by putting your little finger into the corner of their mouth.

# When Should I Stop the Night Feeds?

**My son is nearly six months old and a healthy weight. Is this about the right age to stop feeding him at night?**

Yes. From about six months babies who are developing well don't need night feeds, so you can start phasing them out. I was really lucky because all three of my kids just started to sleep longer. A lot of people told me to wake them to feed them every four hours and I remember that used to drive my mum mad. She'd say: if they want to sleep, why are you waking them up?

As a general rule, if you're breastfeeding and the night feed is less than five minutes, try stopping it altogether and, when your son wakes up, settle him as you would when you put him down at night. If the night feeds are longer, gradually cut down the time you spend feeding him over several days.

If you're bottle-feeding and your son is having only a little milk (60ml or less) you can stop straightaway. If he has more than that, reduce the milk by 20–30ml every second night until you reach 60ml, then stop. This should gradually wean him off the night feeds and he should start to sleep through.

♥

# Is She Ready for Solid Food?

**My daughter is five months old and I'm thinking of trying her on solid food as she still seems hungry after a feed. Is this the right time to start weaning her off the bottle, and do you have any tips on encouraging her to eat solids?**

Around six months is the recommended time to start introducing solid food – until then breast milk and formula will fulfil all your baby's nutritional needs. All three of my kids were around this age when I started giving them solids.

As your baby is still only five months, you could try offering more milk at each feed first to see how that goes. However, if you feel strongly your baby is ready for solids now, why not check with your health visitor or GP? It's important not to give solid food to babies before they're four months old as it's thought to increase their risk of having allergies and getting infections. When babies get to six months, though, they need more than just milk and, at this age, they are able to sit up with support and move food around their mouths. Their digestive and immune systems are also stronger.

Now for the fun part! Once you've decided to make the leap into feeding her solids, you have to accept it's going to get messy. From now on puréed food will literally end up smeared or splattered on every available surface, so have a damp cloth handy!

It's important not to rush her – go at her pace, as it'll probably take a bit of time for her to get used to this strange sensation. You might get a few tears and refusals, but instead of forcing her to eat if she's becoming unhappy, just try again next time and keep persevering until she gets used to it. Some people suggest getting babies started on solids by mixing a little puréed food – such as banana, carrot or cooked apple – with a teaspoon of breast milk or formula. It's OK to give them mashed-up family food as long as it doesn't have any salt, sugar or honey added to it.

For more information on how to wean your baby and what to feed her, visit the Food Standards Agency website: www.eatwell.gov.uk. Good luck!

♥

## I Can't Bond With My Baby

**I had my son ten months ago but I don't seem able to bond with him properly. I know I should be excited about being a mum, but I'm not. I feel I no longer have a life and when he cries I panic about what to do and fear I'm not good enough to take care of him.**

**I seem to have spent the past ten months crying and I'm too scared to talk to anyone – including my partner – in case they tell me I'm a bad mum. What should I do?**

You're showing signs of postnatal depression (PND), but don't for one minute feel this makes you a bad mother. The good thing is that you've realized something isn't right.

The first thing to understand is that these symptoms are much more common than you think – I have several friends who have gone through this. The second thing to understand is that PND is temporary and you will get better. The next step is to talk about it. Years ago, it used to be a case of, 'Don't be silly, get on with it!' but there is a great deal of help available now.

Start by talking to your partner. He's probably noticed something is wrong and you may be surprised by how understanding he is. Perhaps he can come to the doctor with you. That way he can see it's a medical condition and you can discuss ways of dealing with it together. It will also help you to have a name for what you're going through, so you'll be reassured you're not a bad mum.

With PND it's common to have symptoms that include feelings of hopelessness and despair, overwhelming tiredness, an inability to cope, irrational fears for your health or your baby's health, blaming your partner or your baby for how you feel, anxiety and panic attacks. Making a recovery is often as simple as getting practical help from family and friends so you can cope at home. Once you feel you're more in control and are managing things better, the depression lifts.

Your GP might prescribe you antidepressants for a while

and/or refer you for counselling or cognitive behavioural therapy to talk through your feelings, help counter negative thoughts and teach you coping skills.

I'm also a big believer in talking to other mums who've been through this and come out the other side. It'll be good for you to find out how they coped and see that there is light at the end of the tunnel. You'll find plenty of online forums where you can chat to other mums. Meet-a-Mum Association (www.mama.co.uk) was set up to help new mums who feel depressed and isolated after the birth and runs local groups round the country where mums can meet. The National Childbirth Trust (www.nct.org.uk) can also put you in touch with a group of mums local to you.

My friends with PND all sought help and they're now feeling fine – and once the depression was under control, bonding with their babies came naturally. I know it will for you, too.

## Meeting Other New Mums

There's no doubt that becoming a mum can be isolating, particularly if you're the first among your group of friends to have a baby. Suddenly your social life stops and you can go a whole day without having a grown-up conversation! I enjoyed going to a local mother and baby group because it was a chance to get out of the house and have a cup of tea with people who understood what I was going through. I was able to share my worries with the other mums and get good tips, too. If you're desperate to make new mum friends . . .

- Ask at your doctor's surgery or library about local groups where you can meet other mums or find out from your health visitor if there are any post-natal groups in your area.
- Contact the National Childbirth Trust (www.nct.org.uk), which has local branches throughout the country offering support as well as events and activities for new parents.
- Get out and about with the buggy – chatting to other mums in the park with babies of a similar age is a great way to make friends.
- If getting out of the house is still hard, look for online forums where new mums can chat. Try www.netmums.com and www.mumsnet.com.
- Take your baby to classes. Leisure centres and gyms offer baby swimming classes usually from three months. Or try baby yoga or baby massage courses.

♥

# I Worry My Baby Isn't Developing As He Should

**I'm a first-time mum with a seven-month-old son. I should really be enjoying this time, but all I keep worrying about is whether he's developing normally for his age. I'm always comparing him to my friends' babies, who have already started to crawl and shuffle around on their bottoms, but he's not interested. Am I being overanxious?**

When I had Shane Junior I was always trying to push him on to the next milestone – I remember being desperate for him to crawl, then walk and talk. As a first-time parent I was just so excited about seeing him reach all these new stages. But some babies take longer to reach milestones than others, which doesn't necessarily mean there's anything to worry about. I'm sure if you talked to a big group of mums you'd find their children all learnt to do things at slightly different ages. One child might learn to walk earlier than his friends, but could be much slower at learning to talk.

Shane started to walk early – he was about ten months old when he took his first steps. Jake was about a year old, but that's probably because I never pushed him. I wasn't quite ready for him to start running around!

I don't think you have anything to worry about yet, but if

you're spending a lot of time being stressed about your son instead of enjoying the first year of his life, make an appointment with your GP soon to talk it over. You probably just need some reassurance to put your mind at rest. If the doctor does think it's a good idea to check his development, though, it'll be good you've raised your concerns early. Here are some milestones to look forward to in your baby's first year. Remember though, the time it takes for each baby to reach a milestone varies from one child to another, so this is just intended as a rough guide.

- **In the first few weeks** you'll be treated to that first smile. They'll also move around more, kick, swipe at toys and grasp people's fingers. You should also be starting to get to know their personality a little – when they're content or grumpy.
- **At three months** they'll laugh and make other noises such as gurgles and squeals to let you know how they feel. They should also be able to hold their head steady and might even do a mini push-up.
- **At five months** they should start to roll over, may recognize their own name and can amuse themselves by playing with their hands and feet. Stranger anxiety may set in and they'll by comforted by you being there.
- **At six months** they'll be able to roll over in both directions and start to imitate sounds. They may also start to sit

momentarily without support and you should expect lots of jabbering baby talk!

- **At seven to eight months** they should sit without support and be able to lunge forwards or crawl. They should also be able to pass objects from hand to hand.
- **At nine to twelve months** you should hear those words you've been longing to hear: Mama and Dada! They will point at things they want, be able to wave goodbye and pick up small objects and put them into containers. They'll also be crawling well, pulling themselves up and side-stepping along the furniture. They may be able to stand alone for a few seconds and, by twelve months, could be taking their first steps.

Remember every baby is different but you might want to talk to your GP if your baby is having trouble:

- raising their head by three months
- sitting without support by nine months
- using gestures such as pointing by a year old

## I Can't Stop Him Putting Things in His Mouth

**My one-year-old keeps picking up everything he finds and putting it in his mouth. Yesterday it was a flower. I live in fear of him choking on something when I'm not looking. I can give him his dummy, but I want to wean him off that soon.**

This is such a common problem and something all kids go through. My advice would be to let your son keep sucking his dummy. At one, he's still young – my kids kept using theirs till they were two – and at least that way he has something in his mouth to distract him. I think mums can be put under too much pressure to wean their child off a dummy. Don't bow to it. I can relate to how nervous you must feel, though. It's every parent's nightmare that their child might choke on something, and you live in fear of it. I've been through it with all three of mine.

However, at your son's age, it's normal for him to want to put things in his mouth. It's to do with teething and curiosity – it's a natural reflex. All you can do is be vigilant and, if he ever is crawling about on his own, make sure all the small things he could potentially choke on are out of the way. He will grow out of it – usually between eighteen months and two years – and you'll notice he'll start to keep things in his hands rather than put them in his mouth. If I were you, I'd stick with the dummy until that starts to happen. That way, you at least will feel better.

## Coping With Over-Helpful Grandparents

It's a dilemma all new mums face – your parents or in-laws are desperate to be involved with the baby and have lots of advice on how you *should* be doing things. The trouble is you want to do things *your* way.

In my experience, the key to keeping everybody happy is to learn to compromise and pick your battles very carefully. Because, let's face it, you need their support.

I have to admit, when I had Shane Junior, both sets of parents were fantastic – I could always call them if I was worried about the baby. Just to hear them say, 'He's fine, he probably just needs winding' or 'Why don't you try this or that?' was massively reassuring.

Problems can arise because it's been decades since they had

babies and some ideas have moved on. I remember when Shane was teething my mum would say, 'Just put a bit of whisky on his gums and he'll be fine!' because that's what she used to do. Whisky on his gums! 'Do you think I'm going to give my baby whisky?' I'd shriek back. And of course the reply was always, 'Well it didn't do you lot any harm.' So advice like that I just chose to ignore. But other advice was invaluable, so I always let her have her say and if it was something I didn't agree with, I just wouldn't do it.

One thing I'll always be grateful to my mum for was helping me not to become a neurotic or overprotective mum. You know the sort who's always chasing after her kids with an antibacterial wipe? My mum used to say, 'Let them play and get dirty hands, we can wash them afterwards. A little bit of dirt won't do them any harm.' I still think that's a good attitude to have.

Mothers-in-law can be trickier to handle than your own mum because it's easier to fall out with them. I got on brilliantly with Shane's mum when Shane Junior was little and she really helped out with childcare when I was working. But we did have a few minor power struggles. I'd say to her, 'This is his routine,' and she'd reply, 'Well, when he's with me, he'll fit into my routine,' and I'd think, 'Uh, oh!' I thought about it for a while and decided that she was doing me a favour, so the baby had to fit in with her lifestyle. There were lots of other little incidents, like when Shane was a bit older and she took him to get his hair cut. At the time there was a style called the Step, which I loathed, so I asked her not to let Shane have it. And of course, he came home with the Step! But after I calmed down, I thought, 'You know what, his hair will grow back. Is it really worth causing a big row over?' Occasionally, I'd ask Shane to have a word with his mum about certain things because I thought she'd be less likely to fall out with him, but he never wanted to do it. And, at the end of the day, she was a brilliant help, so I decided it was up to me to button my lip over things that weren't important enough to risk falling out over.

It is easy, though, for a situation to spiral into a battle of the wills if your style of parenting is very different to that of your mum or mother-in-law. If you're the kind of mum who never gives your kids sweets, but your parents are constantly feeding them rubbish, it can get very frustrating. But take a leaf out of my book and take some time to think about the situation before you react. Your child might be given chocolate for an afternoon, but they're with you most of the time and they'll be eating what you want them to eat.

Ultimately, grandparents are a great help and you can't pick and choose when you'll need them and how you'd like them to behave. The last thing you want to do is hurt their feelings so they say they don't want to babysit again. In my experience there aren't many situations where you can't reach a compromise.

# How Can I Stop My Mum Spoiling Him With Sweets?

**My mum keeps giving sweets to my one-year-old son, even though I've asked her not to. I know it's just because she loves him and wants to give him a treat, but now all he wants is chocolate instead of his usual healthier snacks. How can I get her to stop without upsetting her?**

First of all, sit down and have a chat to her about it – she might not realize it's upsetting you so much. There's no need to be confrontational, just start by saying, 'I really appreciate all your help, Mum, but I'm trying to make sure he eats healthily at the moment. I'm counting on you to help me out.'

She's just spoiling him a bit, like most grandparents. Why not let her give him an occasional treat, but emphasize that for most of the time he needs to stick to his healthier snacks.

If your son is with your mum a lot and she continues to give him sweets behind your back, though, you're entitled to be annoyed. You need to explain that these are the rules you follow at home and she ought to respect that. But I'm convinced that once your mum realizes how important this is to you, she'll stop. And, after all, there are plenty of other ways she can treat her grandson without giving him sweets.

# Who Should Care for My Baby When I Go Back to Work?

**I'm going back to work soon but I still can't make up my mind about whether to put my eleven-month-old daughter into a nursery or leave her with a childminder. I think she's too young for nursery but I'm worried she might start to love a child-minder more than me and I'll feel jealous of the bond between them.**

This is such a common worry for mums: the thought of going back to work and leaving your child, fearing they might forget about you or not love you as much as someone else. But I can guarantee this won't happen. You'll always be your daughter's mum and no matter who she's left with, she'll always have that incredible unconditional love for you.

Whichever option you go for, it's going to be a wrench. But you'll find a solution that suits you and your daughter if you do your homework properly to find out what's available in your local area. A recommendation from other mums is a good way to start – if they are pleased with how a nursery or child-minder is caring for their children and their little ones are happy, that's very reassuring. And trust your gut instinct, too. When visiting a nursery ask yourself if it offers the standard and style of care you would be happy with. Do the children look stimulated and content? Are the staff happy? Is it a nice environment for the kids? You should also be confident the building is safe and secure.

The benefit of going for a registered childminder is that they have fewer children to care for (up to six) and so can offer your baby more one-to-one time. It's a good sign if they belong to the National Childminding Association – you can search for your nearest childminder on www.ncma.org.uk. The childminder should offer you a contract. Check out extra costs such as nappies and outings upfront. Make sure her home is child-friendly and watch how she reacts to your baby – if you're not totally happy, say no. In England childminders are registered with Ofsted, in Scotland with the Scottish Commission for the Regulation of Care and in Wales, the Care and Social Services Inspectorate.

Good luck!

# Help! I Feel Like a Bad Mum – I'm Going Back to Work

Juggling work with being a mum isn't easy. From the minute your baby is born you have this instant love for them – along with instant guilt! And that never leaves you. Shane Junior is twenty-one and I still feel guilty every time I'm not there for something. It's an in-built emotion.

The key is to focus on all the benefits your work brings you and your family. The main one being you can give your kids a better standard of living. If you enjoy working, you'll feel fulfilled and that will make you a happier mum.

Here are a few things I've learnt from being a working mum myself and from the other mums I've met:

- **Get into a routine.** If you're returning to work after a break, the first couple of weeks will be the hardest as your child will probably be clingy and might worry you won't be coming home. But as soon as you get into a regular routine, they'll know Mummy is back at tea time and they'll get used to it. And when you see how they adapt, you'll feel happier, too.
- **Rise above negative comments.** You'll come across some

people who feel it's wrong to work if you have young children and who don't mind telling you either! I tend to think that's all well and good if you win the Lottery, but how else are you supposed to pay the bills? The main thing is that your kids feel loved and secure.

- **Spend quality time with them.** Enjoy the time you do have with your kids. Does it really matter if you make them fish-fingers and baked beans for tea some nights if it means you have more time to do something nice together? I don't think so – they'll survive!
- **Be proud you're a good role model.** Get your kids interested in your job and explain why you do it. They'll soon be asking you loads of questions.
- **Rope in friends and family.** I'm lucky because Ray works from home a lot and he can take care of Ciara when I'm not there. But if you find yourself in a sticky situation with work and need someone to help out, lean on the grandparents or your mates. If nothing else, you'll find out who your real friends are!
- **Make the job work for you.** If you want to be around at certain times for your kids, ask about flexitime. Or if it's more of a work/life balance you're after, ask yourself if you could afford to do a job share with someone or work part-time. Maybe you have the type of job where you could work from home some days? Don't be shy of asking your employer what's available to you.

# How Do I Tell Them a New Baby's Coming?

**I've just found out I'm pregnant and I'm worried how my older children, who are both at school, will take the news. Have you any advice?**

Before Ciara was born Jake had had me to himself for nine years and was used to being the youngest in the family and my 'baby'. He used to say things like, 'I'd run away from home if you had a baby.'

When I found out I was pregnant, I tested the water a bit by saying things like: 'Would you really be angry if I got pregnant?' and he told me in no uncertain terms that he would. After about a month I felt I had to tell him. I said calmly, 'Jake, you wouldn't really run away if I was having a baby, would you?' He immediately said, 'Why, are you pregnant?' When I nodded, he just flung his arms round me, full of joy, then ran out of the house and told a stranger on the street: 'My mum's pregnant!'

So, you can worry too much about these things. The main thing is for your children to be involved in the pregnancy. We went shopping for baby clothes together and I got him to make a list of his favourite names.

When Ciara was born, I got into the habit of getting Jake to help me with her so that he didn't feel pushed out. This sometimes meant changing a nappy took thirty minutes, but it was important he felt included. If the baby started crying and I was doing something with Jake, I didn't just drop everything to run to her. I'd let her cry for a bit so Jake knew that it was just as important for me to help him.

♥

## I Worry My Son Will Be Jealous of My New Baby

**I'm pregnant and worried that my two-year-old son is going to get jealous when I bring the baby home. I've heard that the first half-hour my son spends with the baby is crucial. Have you any advice on how to help him adjust?**

Some experts say when you bring your baby home for the first time, it's best not to carry them in your arms, so when your other child sees you together they don't get jealous. Because I was worried how Jake would handle it, when I brought Ciara home she was in a car seat. I think it's a good idea to bring the baby in and then let your other child just sit there, have a look and get used to them.

Your son will have insecurities so reassure him constantly. Involve him as much as you can: ask him to help you make the nursery nice and change nappies.

Your son will probably be excited about the baby to start with, but the novelty usually wears off after a few weeks when he realizes it's just a baby that cries a lot! But sibling rivalry is normal. Don't feel you've failed if your son does get upset. Just give him lots of encouragement so he doesn't feel left out.

## My Three Ways to . . . Prepare Them For a New Brother or Sister

**Don't delay.** Break the news to your children as soon as you can. That way you will have longer to prepare them for the arrival of their new sibling.

**Form a team.** Involve your kids as much as you can in the lead-up to the birth – get them to help with practical things such as choosing a pram and decorating the nursery.

**Share the love.** Once the baby arrives, make sure your other children feel included. Ensure there's always someone sitting with them while you are with the baby. Make it clear they are loved and the new baby isn't a threat.

# Will I Love My New Baby As Much?

**I have an eight-year-old daughter and I've found myself (accidentally!) pregnant again. Although I'm six months pregnant, I haven't spent much time thinking about the new baby and I'm terrified I won't be able to love him or her as much as my daughter. Do all mums feel like this?**

It can be scary when you find yourself pregnant again after there's been a big gap since your last child. As you know, my daughter Ciara came along nine years after Jake and I felt nervous about starting all over again with the night feeds, the nappies and just being plain knackered! But while the practical things might seem daunting, you mustn't worry about loving your baby. Mother Nature will kick in and, when you get that little one placed in your arms for the first time, you'll fall in love and all those worries will slip away.

Your daughter will also be excited about having a new brother or sister. And, at her age, she'll want to help you with things like bath time and feeds, which will help you all to bond.

It's an exciting time, so enjoy it!

TWO

# Clawing Back Some 'Me Time'

# It's All About You!

'Me time! What's that?' I can hear you laugh. Yep, when that first baby comes along, they instantly become the most important person in the house – and that won't change for the next sixteen years at least!

So where does that leave you? Well, clean hair and shaved legs suddenly seem like luxuries, as you cater day and night to your child's needs. You'll forget what it's like to look and feel sexy. Shuffling round the kitchen in a dressing gown that's seen better days is as glamorous as it gets these days, right?

Then there's the effect on your relationship. 'Hmmm . . . wonder if I'll ever have the time (or the inclination) to have sex again?' you ask yourself. There's no getting round it – having kids changes your relationship completely. So it's important to find time for yourself and your partner from the word go. After all, as your kids get bigger they just start making different demands on your time. I know what it's like to think, 'I just can't be bothered. I'm too tired to organize anything.' But you have to remember you're a couple as well as Mum and Dad. When your kids go to school and eventually leave home, all you'll have left will be your relationship, so it's important to pay attention to it now.

There's no doubt that 'me time' is much harder to find when your kids are young. When Ciara was a baby, I made sure I had a sitter once a week so Ray and I could have a date night when we'd go to the pictures and have a meal. Occasionally, I'd get the sitter to stay overnight, which was perfect because we didn't have to rush back. But even a few hours to feel like a couple again is better than nothing. If you can persuade the grandparents to look after the kids for longer, sneak away for a weekend. Even if you don't swing from a single rafter the entire time and all you do is sleep, at least you'll be together!

It's so important for new mums and dads to find some time to be alone. Having a tiny baby can be a danger period for lots of couples – focusing on your new arrival a hundred per cent combined with pure exhaustion can put a strain on even the strongest relationship. All it takes is for one of you to start feeling unappreciated or resentful for communication to break down. Making the effort to have some regular nights out together will help rebuild the closeness and remind you why you fell in love in the first place.

And, remember, whatever age your kids are, it won't harm them if you're away from them for a little while. They may cry when you leave the house, but as soon as you shut the front door they'll be fine – trust me! I remember one evening Shane Junior and Jake screamed the place down when I was on my way out. I felt like the worst mum in the world leaving them, so I nipped round the back and looked through the dining-room window to see if they were OK. Of course, the tears had miraculously dried up and they were happily watching telly with the babysitter!

When you're at home with the kids all day, it's important to have a break, too. When Ciara was a baby I either had a sleep when she went down for a nap or took the opportunity to do something else nice for myself. I'd paint my nails or have a bath or put my feet up and watch a favourite movie with a cuppa. It didn't matter if the house was a wreck; I thought, 'I can tidy up when she's awake.' Your house isn't a movie set, so take that pressure off yourself.

When you become a mum, it's natural to feel you've lost a bit of your identity. I've had loads of letters from mums all saying the same thing: 'All I am now is a wife and a mum. I've forgotten what it's like to be me!' But before you trade your kids in for a life of carefree singledom, there are ways of squeezing in a bit more time for yourself *and* rediscovering the sexy, confident woman you were when you first met your partner.

# How to . . . Help Yourself

**Stop trying to be perfect.** Er, did someone not tell you it's impossible? It's easy to feel you're not good enough when the house is in chaos, but that's what happens if you have young children. Anyone who says your home is messy isn't much of a friend. If you get things 80 per cent right, that'd be good enough to get an A grade on an exam paper – so think of it that way. If you're maintaining a C average, that's pretty good, too. An hour to yourself is often worth more than a tidy living room.

**Delegate!** Cut down the time you spend tidying by getting older kids to help. Give them a few chores to do each week and reward them with a bit of extra pocket money. Or find something they enjoy doing so it doesn't seem as much like a chore. Shane Junior and Jake were never very good at tidying their bedrooms, but they were brilliant at keeping Ciara amused, which gave me a bit of precious time to myself.

**Rope in friends and relatives.** Most grandparents will jump at the chance of spending time with their grandchildren, so work out how they can help you more. Could they pick up the kids after school or nursery, or could they take them to swimming lessons or football at weekends? As long as you're not abusing their good nature, they should be happy to help. You should also get together with friends who have kids and set up a babysitting pool or suggest taking turns on the school run.

**Learn to say 'no'.** Us mums are often people pleasers, but you can say 'no' without being a bad person. Your time is precious, so if someone asks you to do something, make sure it's something you really want to do before committing to it.

**Get clever with cleaning.** Try to tidy as you go along: wash up as you're making the tea, for example, so you don't have to face a huge pile of dirty dishes afterwards. And allocate time during the week to give different parts of the house a proper clean – don't try to do the whole place in one go. By doing the cleaning in small chunks you'll keep on top of it more easily and it won't seem as daunting. Get into a routine of doing the cleaning in the same order – you'll soon speed up and get it done more quickly.

# My Instant Glamorizers

Busy mums don't have loads of spare time to spend in beauty salons – you're lucky to find five minutes to brush your hair some days – but looking good doesn't have to be a major operation. I remember when I had Shane Junior I felt such a frump, but I made sure I put on a bit of lippy and mascara every afternoon without fail – it only took a couple of minutes and it made me feel better. After years of being a working mum and juggling a hundred things at once, I've learnt lots of quick and easy tricks that'll help you feel glam and boost your body confidence.

- **Get fitted for a bra.** Don't laugh! Most of us wear the wrong size, leaving our boobs less than perky. But I promise, the right bra will lift your bust and make you look slimmer in five seconds flat. I should know – I need scaffolding to keep my huge breasts in the right place! Department stores like John Lewis and Marks & Spencer have a free bra-fitting service.
- **Dye your lashes.** Even if you have dark lashes, the tips of them are fair, so getting them dyed makes a huge difference. They'll look instantly longer and thicker – and you won't

have to bother with mascara. Visit a salon or dye them yourself at home. Boots stocks home lash and brow dye kits. Try Eyelure Dylash 45 Day Mascara.

- **Get waxed.** No time to shave or pluck? Get unwanted body hair waxed off and you won't have to worry about it for weeks. An eyebrow wax takes about ten minutes, but it gives your whole face a lift and you look groomed in an instant.
- **Have your make-up done.** Next time you're doing your shopping without the kids, visit a department store beauty counter and get your make-up done for free. Why not time it to coincide with a night out?
- **Use multi-tasking beauty products.** Hard-working beauty products are a must for time-starved mums. Vaseline does virtually everything – it's a great treatment for dry skin, it's a lip balm, slick it on your eyebrows to shape them or use it to take off make-up (it's gentle but gets rid of the most stubborn mascara), and it's cheap as chips. Use hair conditioner as a shave cream for your legs and baby wipes as make-up remover. Johnson's Baby Lotion is a great body moisturiser and make-up remover. And try a make-up stick like Nars Multiple, which is a blusher, eyeshadow and lip tint all in one.
- **Try figure-fixing underwear.** OK, it might not look too sexy, but who cares if it makes you look like you've lost half a

stone and gives you an hourglass figure for a night out? These days there's everything from waist-cinchers and thigh-slimming shorts to all-in-ones that smooth every lump and bump. Marks & Spencer's Magic range does the trick and it's pretty, too. Visit www.marksandspencer.com.

## Rediscovering Romance

Your love life is usually the first thing to suffer when kids come along and it's easy to forget you once fancied each other! Here are some ideas on how to relight the fire.

- **Have a date night.** Recapture that feeling you had when you were first seeing each other by going on regular dates – it doesn't matter if it's once a week, once a fortnight or once a month. Get dressed up and meet your partner there to make it more exciting. It's a chance to spend some proper grown-up time together.
- **Stay home alone.** Pack the kids off to your parents' so you can spend the night at home alone. Get a takeaway, have a glass of wine, watch a movie, then head to bed! Make sure you have a lovely long lie-in the next morning.
- **Keep in touch.** Send text messages during the day telling

him how much you're looking forward to your night together or how much you fancy him. It's romantic and it'll build the excitement, so hopefully you'll be ripping each other's clothes off as soon as you get through the front door!

- **Make the bedroom a technology-free zone.** Your bedroom is for sleep and sex – so get rid of all those distractions like TVs and computers.
- **Don't save sex till bedtime.** Let's be honest, when you get into bed at night, you're often too exhausted to contemplate sex, so set the alarm a little earlier and make love in the morning – it'll put a smile on your face for the rest of the day! Or take the opportunity during the day when the baby is having a nap.
- **Do nice things for each other.** Don't wait for birthdays to give each other treats. Buy him that CD he wants and leave it on his pillow. Give him a thrill with some sexy new lingerie – if you're embarrassed by your control pants and grey bra, they won't be doing much for him, either! Hopefully, he'll get the message and think of some ways to put a smile on your face, too.

THREE

# Tricky Toddlers and Pre-Schoolers

# Toddler Taming Time!

Toddlers are fantastic – they're developing their little personalities, walking, talking, learning new things every day and they're absolutely hilarious. It's a really rewarding time for mums, but it can be pure hell, too! They're not quite old enough to reason with and, because they can't communicate sensibly with you, it either turns into a tantrum or they just keep doing the same thing over and over again that you've told them a hundred times not to do. They're trying to assert themselves, but, just as with puppies, you have to let them know who's leader of the pack! And that's Mum.

At times, when my boys were really little, they absolutely ruled me. So I know from experience that if you let them get away with things once, you're making a rod for your own back. But it's hard when you're at home with them all day. Sometimes I'd be so sick of constantly telling them 'No' all day, I'd suddenly find myself saying, 'Just drink the shampoo, I'm not bothered! As long as you're happy and you shut up for ten minutes.' But you find out that's not going to get you anywhere because they learn you'll always give in.

Then there's the unpredictability factor. I've heard so many stories from mums who've been put in the most embarrassing situations by their toddlers. One mum told me her little girl pulled down her pants in the middle of a really posh restaurant and weed on the floor! Another mum said her little girl went through a phase of shouting, 'Why is that lady fat?' whenever she saw an overweight woman. And I remember being in a shop with Jake one day when he suddenly decided to take all his clothes off.

But probably the worst case for me was a trip to the Early Learning Centre with Shane when he was about three-and-a-half and I was really heavily pregnant with Jake. I'd taken him there to get some Plasticine because he'd been going mad for it, but, of course, once he got inside the shop and saw all the other toys, Plasticine wasn't enough. He ended up pulling a whole shelf down and was still hanging on to it as I was trying to drag him away. Picture the scene: I'm a week overdue with Jake and massive. I've got the buggy laden with shopping and I'm trying to peel Shane's hands off the shelf while he's screaming blue murder. Eventually I got him out of the shop and into the buggy, but he got out of the pram, threw himself on the ground and started screaming hysterically. Convinced I was about to go into labour at any moment, I just stepped over him and an old lady said, 'Oh, that's a shame.' I snapped back, 'Don't even go there!'

Finally in the car, I sobbed all the way home. And of course Shane was sobbing too, saying he was sorry. But at that point sorry just wasn't enough. I couldn't even talk to him. When I got home I told my sister I couldn't even look at him because I didn't love him at that moment. Then I ended up sobbing again because I felt so guilty about feeling that way.

Yes, it can be hard, exhausting and frustrating, but then two hours after they've thrown the tantrum to end all tantrums in front of your mother-in-law, they do something absolutely fantastic and you know you wouldn't change it for the world.

# Can Dummies Lead to Bad Teeth?

**Is it a myth that dummies lead to dental problems later in childhood? My two-and-a-half-year-old still uses his.**

No, it's not a myth – dentists say the longer your child uses a dummy, the more chance there is of it changing the shape of their mouth inside, which can affect how their teeth meet when biting. One thing you should never do is dip their dummy into anything sweet like honey or fruit juice, as it leads to tooth decay.

At your son's age you should be trying to stop him regularly using his dummy. One of the best things I did was take Ciara to the dentist when she was about two-and-a-half. He had a chat with her and said, 'Will you be a good girl and stop using your dummy? That way you'll grow up and have beautiful teeth.' He also explained how much prettier she'd look with nice teeth and that if she brushed them twice a day, they'd be strong and healthy. He gave her a badge and a special toothbrush and she was delighted.

I used to turn teeth brushing into a game, saying things like 'I bet my teeth are shinier than yours' to encourage them to brush. Kids love a good contest.

## My Three Ways to . . . Get Your Toddler to Give up the Dummy

**Be strong.** When you make the decision you'll get tears, but don't give in. When we decided it was time for Ciara to ditch her dummy, she pleaded to have it back, but once she got through that first night she was fine.

**Don't give in.** Remember, the moment you give in you'll be back to square one. Keep it up and be prepared for a few sleepless nights. My son Jake cried for his dummy for three nights, but after that we never looked back.

**Make a fuss of them.** Tell relatives and friends that your child is giving up their dummy in front of them. Say, 'She's getting rid of her dummy, isn't she grown-up?' Or try saying, 'You're big now and other little children need your dummy.'

# He Hates His 'New' Bed!

**I've just taken the sides off my three-year-old son's cot to change it into a bed and he doesn't like it. He doesn't get out of the bed, he just wakes up five times a night shouting for me! He says he wants the sides back on. What should I do?**

It sounds like he's feeling insecure. He probably looks around and sees this big, open space. It seems a small thing to us, but it's a big step for them. Ciara was fine when I put her into a 'big' bed – I was the one going in five times a night to check on her! She looked so small.

You can buy fabulous bed guards now to stop them rolling out of bed. They don't run the full length of the bed – just at the head end, so your child can still get out if he wants to. I bought one for Ciara. It gives them security and also gives you peace of mind. When Ciara got older I put a pillow lengthways next to her, so if she moved she'd feel safe.

Keep reassuring your son – tell him what a big boy he is now he's sleeping in a big bed so he feels special and grown-up.

## My Three Ways to . . . Stop Them Getting Into Your Bed at Night

**Be consistent.** It can be a long, hard slog trying to convince a toddler to stay in their own bed. Although it's tempting to give in and let them snuggle up, every time they try it, get up and lead them by the hand back to their own room.

**Make it cosy.** There's probably a reason why your child keeps getting up in the night. Maybe they're a bit scared. Try a night light to make it less frightening and daunting. Or perhaps a new teddy or a hot-water bottle will help.

**If you give in you'll be even more tired!** No matter how often it happens, you have to keep putting them back to bed. It's exhausting getting up each time, but if you don't nip it in the bud, who knows how long it'll go on for.

# Potty Training Made Easy . . . Yes, Really!

This is a traumatic time for all mums. Cleaning up those little puddles of wee that appear all over the house isn't much fun. What I've realized, having had three kids, is that they all react differently to potty training.

Shane got to a point where he'd wee on the potty but only poo in a nappy. And Jake was a nightmare – he'd poo in his pull-up pants, then take them off before I could get to him. There would be poo everywhere! We had a golden retriever at the time, who would then walk the poo all over the house. I remember Jake standing there one day, covered from his waist down in poo. He was trying to toddle about, while I'm screaming at him to stand still, then thinking, 'Oh God, I have to pick him up now with all this poo on him!'

Ciara, on the other hand, was a dream – she never had a potty. We went on holiday to Turkey when she was two-and-a-half and it was boiling hot, so I left her nappy off and told her to tell me when she needed the toilet. From that day on, she'd run to thc loo when she needed to go. She just got it.

The trouble with potty training is that just when you think

you've cracked it, it goes horribly wrong and you're back to square one. But don't give up – there are a few golden rules that should make things a little easier. Good luck!

- **Make sure they're ready.** Most children learn to use a potty around their second birthday. They could be ready if they're staying dry for a couple of hours a day, have a poo at regular times and can let you know if they need their nappy changed.
- **Avoid stressful times.** Don't start potty training if there are other big events happening in your lives such as a new baby or a house move.
- **Be positive.** Make using the potty seem exciting and grown-up. Say, 'You're so grown-up using the potty!' Maybe get them to help pick out a potty so they feel involved from the start.
- **Give lots of praise.** When they manage to wee or poo in the potty, tell them how good they've been. Toddlers really respond to praise and want to impress you.
- **Put them in the right clothes.** Clothes that can either be pulled up or pulled down quickly are the key. Think elasticated waists instead of rows of fiddly buttons.
- **Try training pants.** These are useful at first to cope with those little accidents.
- **Don't force them.** If you try to force them to sit on the potty, they might get upset and it just makes the process more difficult.

- **Reward them.** Don't give sweets, but reward them instead with gold stars to stick on a wall chart or let them watch their favourite DVD.

♥

## My Two-Year-Old Still Wants a Bottle

**My daughter has just turned two and still likes a bottle in the afternoons and before she goes to bed. If she doesn't get it she screams the place down! How can I wean her off it and encourage her to use a cup?**

I don't think your daughter is any different from lots of other toddlers her age – having a bottle, particularly at bedtime, is a comfort and part of her relaxing wind-down before sleep. However, she doesn't need it for nutrition any more and constantly sucking on a bottle could damage her teeth. The key is to stick to your guns once you've made the decision to wean her off it – even if you get tantrums from hell! Here are a few ideas . . .

- **Offer a cup of milk instead before every bottle.** She might refuse it, but even if she takes the odd one instead of a bottle, it's a good start.
- **Do it gradually.** Start cutting the number of bottles she has. For every three feeds, give her a beaker.

- **Praise her.** Even if she only drinks two sips from the beaker; give the most praise you can. Say: 'Wow, you're so grown-up!' And give her lots of cuddles, too.
- **Eliminate her favourite bottle last.** If it's the night feed she likes best, cut this one out last. This will be tough, but persevere and you'll get through it. Eventually she'll learn to fall asleep without it.

## My Three Ways to . . . Get Your Child Talking

**Chat to them.** Whenever possible, talk to them: about what you see when you're walking down the street or tell them what you're doing around the house. There's no normal age for your child to start talking, although most start saying their first words between their first and second birthdays.

**Sing!** Encouraging them to join in nursery rhymes is a good first step towards helping them speak.

**Play games.** Have a tea party or play shops or fire stations. Games like these really encourage them to get talking.

# My Toddler Is So Shy

**My son has just turned three and he's really shy around new people. He started nursery last week and his teacher told me he's been very quiet. What can I do to bring him out of his shell?**

Ciara was the same throughout her first year at nursery school. The teacher said she didn't talk much and kept herself to herself – she was happy to watch others rather than get involved.

But sending shy children to nursery really is the best thing you can do because it helps them gradually to gain confidence. The teachers are experienced at encouraging shy children to do things and involving them in what's going on without them feeling forced. Other kids pick up on their shyness and are good at making friends with them.

Some youngsters are just naturally shy. You can't force your son to be confident – he will come round in his own time. The best thing you can do is to take an interest in what he's doing. When you pick him up from nursery, ask him what he's been doing that day and give him lots of praise – kids like to impress you at that age. Your son is only three so he has plenty of time to grow out of it. Ciara is eight now and you can't shut her up

– she's always up at the front of the class. Don't worry too much. Personally, I'd rather have a nice, shy child than a bolshie brat any day!

# Help! She Has an Imaginary Friend

**My three-year-old daughter has an imaginary friend she talks to and also blames when things go wrong. She's an only child and I'm worried she's lonely. Is it normal for her to have such an active imagination?**

I don't think you have to worry. My sister had an imaginary friend until she was six: we even had to set a place at the table for her every night and save a seat for her in the car! But she grew out of it – and so will your daughter. If she's being naughty and blaming the friend, then just include the friend in your punishment. Tell her there will be no toys for either of them.

I think it's a sign your daughter is very creative. Once she goes to nursery or school there will be other kids with imaginary friends and the staff will know how to deal with it. She will also start to make real friends, who will replace the imaginary one.

For now, I think you should embrace it rather than try to quash it.

# My Son's Afraid of Birds

**My three-year-old son is scared of birds and it's getting to the point where he's frightened to go outside. What should I do?**

Kids are starting to develop very active imaginations at this age and fears like this are quite common. I'd suggest taking him to a zoo with an aviary where the birds are contained. That way he can get used to them without worrying about them hurting him. The worst thing you can do is drag him outside and say, 'Don't be silly,' because that might cause even bigger problems.

When Ciara was younger, she was afraid of spiders and flies. I think she picked up these fears from my nieces, who get hysterical when they see an insect. From an early age, kids are sensitive to other people's fears. Could he have picked up this fear from you?

The way I handled it with Ciara was to give the spiders and flies names, so they seemed less scary and we'd sit on the floor and talk to them. It actually helped me get over my own fear of spiders. Ciara still doesn't like spiders, but she can cope and she doesn't get hysterical any more. When you're out together and see a bird, remain very calm and talk about how nice they are. If it develops into a more serious phobia and you find his fear is starting to affect how you live your lives, you might need to seek advice from your GP.

I can relate to your son's fear, though. When I was a kid I was afraid of birds – it was the flapping of the wings that got me. I grew out of it and, as your son is only three, he probably will, too.

♥

## Should I Limit His TV Time?

**How many hours of TV do you think I should allow my three-year-old son to watch? My husband thinks it should be only ten minutes a day, but I don't see any harm in letting him watch telly for an hour.**

Ten minutes? Really? Personally, I think an hour a day is fine. As a minimum. I can understand where your husband is coming from, not wanting your child to sit in front of trashy programmes all day and it's important to police what they watch. But I think he's perhaps forgetting how old your son is.

These days there are so many good learning programmes for kids on TV – it doesn't have to be mindless stuff. When Ciara was five, she learnt to count from one to ten and to say 'hello', 'goodbye' and 'thank you' in Spanish just from watching kids' TV. And she learnt social skills, too, like how to be kind to other people.

If you can't agree, you could try to compromise with your

husband. Perhaps at weekends you could have a rule where your son watches less TV and you can do things together as a family.

♥

## How Can I Stop Supermarket Tantrums?

**My three-year-old keeps throwing tantrums in the supermarket. It's embarrassing and has now got to the point where I dread the weekly shop. What can I do?**

It's horrendous when this happens. I used to get it a lot with my boys. You're in such a difficult situation because everyone judges you by how you respond. If you raise your voice while asking your child to stop, people look at you as if you're a murderer! But if you ignore the child, people get annoyed that you're not doing anything about it.

Start as you mean to go on. If you try to quieten them with sweets, you'll start a pattern where they know if they throw a tantrum they'll get a treat. My trick with the boys was to involve them. We played games like 'I Spy' and I'd say to them: 'Who's going to find the peas first?' Shopping is boring for kids, so try to make it fun if you can. Praise them if they find something you've been searching for. I'd also reward Shane and Jake with something like a gingerbread man for being my helpers. Ciara used to love the rides some shops have by the tills, so I'd tell her if she was a good girl, she'd get to have a ride at the end. It only cost a few pence and it was definitely worth it!

## My Seven Ways to Handle Toddler Tantrums

- **Ignore it.** Trying to reason with them or talk them out of it only seems to make the tantrum last longer because you're giving them attention.
- **Never bribe them with sweets to get them to behave.** They'll see these treats as a reward for throwing a wobbly!
- **Distract them.** This is a useful technique, particularly if you're in a public place. Sing a silly song, pull a stupid face or get them interested in something that's going on around them. I did this many times with Shane Junior and Jake!
- **Try a time out.** Sending them to a 'naughty' step or corner will give you and them a chance to calm down. Make sure they know why they've been sent there and don't leave them too long. When the time's up, explain again what it was all

about and let them go off to play. Keep this tactic as a last resort or it'll lose its impact.

- **Keep a cool head.** We're probably all guilty of losing our temper and shouting now and again, but it only makes a stressful situation worse – and it doesn't work. It might shock your toddler into silence the first time you do it, but it won't last. Shouting all the time will either make your child really timid or turn them into a horror who shouts back!
- **Pay them attention when they're good.** Once the tantrum has passed, tell them how much more you love them when they're being good and praise them. Noticing when they do things right and giving them praise has a really positive effect. They'll learn that you take more notice of them when they're good than if they're naughty.
- **Try to work out why they do it.** You never know exactly what's going to set them off, but could they be tired, hungry, frustrated or maybe it's because you're not paying them enough attention?

## Coping With Aggressive Tots

From the age of two, Jake used to get into terrible rages and would even try to batter his big brother! I had to physically pull them apart many times and couldn't leave them alone for more than a few seconds or they'd kill each other. Jake actually idolized Shane, who was about five, but Shane didn't want him anywhere near. Jake would then ruin Shane's game and all hell would break loose.

A lot of Jake's aggression was simply down to him trying to get what he wanted – whether that was attention or a toy that someone else was playing with. If he ever lashed out at Shane or another child, I'd take him aside and say very firmly, 'No pushing or hitting.' I would also show concern for the child he'd hurt to make it clear that his behaviour wouldn't get my attention. Time outs were also effective with Jake – simply taking him out of the situation calmed him down.

Jake's toddler tempers were so bad sometimes I was convinced he was going to grow up to be a mass murderer! I'm happy to report he's grown into a lovely young man.

# How Do I Stop Him Biting?

**My son is eighteen months old and has suddenly started biting people. I've noticed it tends to be when he wants attention. I read that when your child bites you should bite them back so they know how it feels, but that doesn't seem right. What should I do?**

Jake was about the same age as your son when he started biting children at nursery – and he was expelled for it! Someone gave me that same tip, but I think it's wrong and you could risk hurting your child. Instead, I put my teeth gently to his arm and said, 'Do you want Mummy to bite you, too?' If you're not comfortable with that tactic, take away his favourite toy and put it out of reach each time he does it. Or stop him from watching his favourite TV programme. I've found this type of discipline pretty effective. But make sure you stick to it. It's very tempting when your child is behaving like an angel again to give them back their toy, but they soon cotton on to this and the punishment is wasted.

Biting is a hundred per cent about getting attention. If they throw a tantrum you can ignore it, but you can't do that with biting. You need to tackle it straightaway.

## *My Three Ways To . . . Get Them To Share Their Toys*

**Time them.** If both children want to play with the same toy, let one of them have it first while the other plays with something else. Tell them after ten minutes they will have to swap, then make sure they do.

**Stand your ground.** Never give in if one of them has a strop and refuses to share. You have to be consistent.

**Get tough.** If they still can't agree over who has the toy, take it away. Once they realize refusing to share means no one gets the toy, they'll soon start making sure everyone gets a turn!

# My Daughter Hits Other Kids

**My little girl is three-and-a-half and she keeps hitting other kids in the park. The other day I caught her thumping a boy and she's also slapped a girl in her class. How can I make her stop?**

This is a hard one. They always say at this age that you should ignore bad behaviour and reward good behaviour, but if your child is being physically aggressive, you have to nip it in the bud. She's old enough to begin to understand the difference between right and wrong, so the next time she hits another child, act immediately. If she's in the park, don't even give her a warning about her behaviour, just take her home straightaway. If she hits out, she goes home. No ifs, no buts. If she slaps another child at home, confiscate a favourite toy. By repeatedly doing this, you'll teach her that being aggressive ultimately hurts her because something she enjoys is taken away. If she has hit out at class-mates, you need to talk to the teachers at nursery. They will have experienced situations like this many times before and may have some suggestions about dealing with it.

She could be craving attention, or maybe she has yet to learn she has to share with other children. Either way, it's most likely a phase. She'll soon see that bad behaviour gets her nowhere, so try not to worry too much.

# We Argue Over How to Discipline Him

**My husband and I argue constantly about how to discipline our three-year-old. I think he's too strict and he thinks I'm a push-over. I'm worried these arguments are affecting our son. Do you have any advice?**

This is a really common problem. All couples argue about how to bring up their kids and I don't think it'll ever change.

It's essential you don't disagree with your husband in front of your son – kids get very stressed if they see their parents arguing. It also teaches them how to play one parent off against the other and they'll learn who's softer and appeal to them. Always show a united front when your son's there and remind your husband he has to follow this rule, too.

If you think your husband is being a bit strict, have a quiet word later when your son is out of earshot. You could also remind your husband that he was a child once! Dads seem to forget this and tend to be stricter than mums. But it may not be a bad thing that your husband is stricter than you are. When Ray came into my life, Shane and Jake needed a strict adult around. Ray was really consistent with discipline and the boys responded well to it.

When your son's a terrible teen, you'll probably be grateful your husband is hotter on discipline than you are!

## Should You Bribe Your Toddler?

I'm a firm believer that bribery is OK – sometimes. If you're really desperate for your kids to behave for a special event like a wedding, offering a treat like some stickers or a comic if they promise to be good doesn't do any harm. And it works!

Giving treats when they're being naughty or throwing a tantrum to get them to behave is a different story, though. If you do this they'll think that every time they act up they'll get something nice. If you go down this route your little angel will be holding you to ransom at every opportunity.

# She Drew On Our Walls!

**My two-and-a-half-year-old daughter drew all over the walls of our lounge with crayon. My husband thinks it's funny, but I want her to know it's unacceptable behaviour. How can I teach her not to do it again?**

I have to admit, I had a giggle when I read your letter. It reminded me of something that happened to my sister Maureen. My other sister Anne and my niece Amy – who was about three – went to stay with her. She'd recently bought a new dining table and hand-carved chairs with velvet covers. They left Amy in the room alone for a few minutes and when they came back she'd written all over the chairs – in marker pen! The chairs were ruined and had to be re-covered.

The truth is, this is the kind of thing three-year-olds get up to. But if you laugh, your daughter will think it's OK to do it again. So if your husband is going to laugh, he must do it when your daughter's not there. You have to be firm. Tell her she mustn't do it again, and, if she does, make sure you remove her favourite toy or send her to the 'naughty' step or corner for a few minutes. You should also make her help you clean it off so she learns from her mistake. Hopefully, she won't repeat it.

I have to say, she is two, so it was a big mistake leaving her in the room alone with a crayon and a wall – you have to learn, too!

# How to Toddler-Proof Your Home (and Your Life!)

You need eyes in the back of your head to keep track of your child once they start running around. If I turned my head for a second, my boys would be off. Never underestimate a toddler – they have an uncanny knack of getting into anything – so think childproof lids on everything!

Making your home as safe as possible will help avoid accidents and give you some peace of mind. You can buy home safety starter packs cheaply (try www.boots.com), which include socket covers, corner cushions and locks for cupboards, drawers and toilets. You can also buy furniture-securing kits. Try the Great Little Trading Company (www.gltc.co.uk), which has safety equipment for kids, including straps to stop furniture tipping over on them.

You should also:

- Fit locks or safety catches to all windows.
- Position furniture such as beds and sofas away from windows so kids aren't tempted to climb up to reach them.
- Get your kids to help choose a toy box, which will make

clearing up their toys more fun – hopefully it'll mean there will be less mess to trip over.

- Fit a stair-gate to the top and bottom of stairs.
- Keep the landing light on in case your toddler gets out of bed during the night.
- Keep chemicals, cleaning fluids, medicines, kitchen knives and anything else hazardous out of reach – and out of sight!
- Keep kettle and toaster flexes away from the edge of kitchen worktops to prevent your kids pulling them over.
- Never leave food unattended when you're cooking on the hob.

♥

## My Son Loves Girls' Toys

**My three-year-old son is obsessed with girly things. He'd always choose a pink duvet cover over a blue one and likes girls' toys, too. Should I try to force him to play with boys' things or could this just be a phase?**

I went through exactly the same thing with Jake – although he'll kill me for saying so! He was like that until he was about four. One Christmas all he wanted was a doll's house and a baby buggy! It never bothered me, but I remember his dad saying, 'I'm not buying my son a doll's house!' Jake loved it, though, and he used to come shopping with me with his doll in a buggy. Once we were in the chemist's and he wanted a teddy with a pink bobble on its ear, so I bought it for him. Then he wanted me to put the bobble in his hair. When we left the shop, a man held a door open for us and said, 'That doesn't look good.' But Jake grew out of it and now he couldn't be more of a lad.

I think lots of mums experience this with their sons when they're little. It could be that the girls' things just look nicer because they usually come in brighter, more attractive colours. Or maybe he is close to you and just wants to be like you? He's only three, so just let him express himself. It's only society that dictates certain things are for boys and others for girls. There isn't the same fuss if a girl is a tomboy and would rather get mucky with the boys than play with dolls. You might find that he loses interest in girly things when he starts mixing with more boys his own age at school.

But, at the end of the day, your son is going to be the person he is no matter which toys he's given to play with, so try not to worry about it.

# Could My Toddler Be a Model?

**People keep commenting how beautiful my two-year-old son is and friends have said I should try to get him into child modelling. It sounds exciting and something he could look back on in years to come, but I'm worried it might be tough. Am I being silly?**

No, I don't think you're being silly. You should definitely find out more about it.

These days, as long as you sign up with a reputable agency, there are strict rules to protect children – for example how many hours they can work in a day.

What you do need to think about is your son's character. Will he be happy doing it? If he's at a photoshoot and he's not happy, it won't matter how good-looking he is, he'll get the chop! I remember when Shane Junior did a sketch in his dad's show when he was two – it got to the third take and he was whimpering and I stepped in and said, 'No more.' My protective instinct kicked in and I couldn't bear to see him looking so tired, so I picked him up and took him away. They were very good about it – and a good agency will react in the same way.

If he does enjoy it, though, that's great. If I were you, I'd put the money he earns aside in an account for him for when he's older. Then it's something he can appreciate later.

# I'm Embarrassed By Her Head Lice

**My four-year-old has head lice and I feel really embarrassed about it. I'm worried about telling the nursery in case the other mothers think my daughter is dirty. How can I get rid of them quickly?**

There's absolutely nothing to be embarrassed about. Head lice are very common. In fact I've caught them three or four times from my children. You must tell the nursery, though, to prevent a big outbreak. There are rules now that nurseries aren't allowed to say which child has it, so your daughter won't be singled out. They will just inform parents there's been a case of it, so everyone can take steps to prevent kids passing it round. The truth is, nits thrive on clean hair, so if people did think your daughter is dirty, they'd be wrong.

There are plenty of good treatments available at the chemist, but they only kill off the ones that have already hatched, so you also have to remove the eggs with a nit comb. Try putting on loads of conditioner to make this easier and repeat in a few days. I ended up getting my hairdresser over to help me and Ciara – I live in a house of men and none of them would do it for us! Remember, you have to treat everyone in the house. If your daughter has long hair, tie it up for nursery so she's less likely to catch them again.

# 'Mummy, He Said the F-word!' What to Do When Toddlers Swear

When my boys were little, there were lots of older kids around and they did pick up swear words. There was one hysterical time when Jake ran in saying Shane had said the F-word, followed closely by Shane sobbing, 'I didn't, I told him to f*** off!' The shock on everyone's faces was priceless. We all fell about laughing!

The key is not to overreact when they swear or they'll learn it's a good way to get your attention. Being angry with them still means they've caught your attention. Here's how to tackle it.

- Explain the word they used isn't nice and ask them not to use it again. I'd also refuse to play with my boys if they swore – they didn't like that at all.
- If they're using a word because their little friend does, tell them if they keep saying it you won't let them play with that child again.
- If they say a rude word when they're angry or hurt, suggest a different, non-offensive word they can use instead.

# How Can I Stop Her Nightmares?

**My four-year-old keeps having nightmares. Is there anything I can do to make her more relaxed at bedtime?**

When Ciara was four, she used to get nightmares, too. It seems to be quite a common age for this, perhaps because they've started or are about to start school and their brains are more active. I remember Ciara used to always be racing round playing hide and seek with her brothers before bedtime and I think this was making her mind race, too. Now I make sure she's as relaxed as possible before bed.

It's important to have a wind-down routine before your child goes to bed – the same as you would with a baby to get them to settle at night. An hour before her bedtime, I'd stop Ciara watching telly and give her a relaxing bath, then I'd tuck her up and read her a couple of nice stories – nothing with wicked witches in them! A routine like this should help your daughter feel calm before bed. If Ciara had a nightmare, I'd go in and reassure her. If she was screaming in her sleep, I'd quietly talk to her.

The one thing you mustn't do is let her come into your bed to sleep – she'll sleep soundly, but you won't!

# How Can I Encourage Her To Be Tidier?

**I'm trying to teach my four-year-old to start being tidier with her belongings. Do you have any suggestions on how I should go about this?**

I remember going through the same thing with Ciara when she was about five.

When she asked if she could get her dolls out, I'd say: 'Yes, but you have to put your other toys away first.' Sometimes she'd do it and other times she'd whine that she was too tired.

The most important thing is to give plenty of encouragement. Lavish her with praise. I'd say: 'You're such a big help to Mummy, I don't know what I'd do without you.' Make sure she feels she's doing something important and that she's acting like a big girl by helping. Children feel so proud if they get that kind of praise from their parents.

You do have to be strict, though. If your daughter complains, emphasize that it means she won't be able to get her toys out again later or tomorrow. It's difficult to be firm in these situations but it really pays off in the long run. The other thing you can do is help when she's putting things away. If she's being difficult, say: 'Well, let's do it together then.' I'd pick up a couple of things but make sure she'd do most of it. It's simply a training process.

You'll get there in the end. Your daughter is very young and she's still learning.

FOUR

# The Diet War

# Yes, You Can Be a Slim and Sexy Mum!

I get loads of letters from mums desperate to lose their baby weight and, God, do I know how they feel!

I was huge when I was pregnant with each of my three of my kids. When I had Shane Junior I was only twenty-three and a few months later I went back to work, doing a two-and-a-half-hour show with the Nolans every night, so the weight fell off easily. But after I had Jake and Ciara I had a real battle on my hands to get my figure back. When you become a mum, it's so easy to forget about yourself. When my kids were babies, I was so busy running round after them that I'd eat on the run, grabbing fattening snacks like crisps, chocolate bars and biscuits to keep my energy levels up. Then as they got older, I'd finish their leftovers, raid the cupboards for their sweets and eat half the dinner while I was cooking it!

It's so easy for the weight to creep on without you even noticing and, before you know it, you've piled on three stone and feel like a big unsexy blob. Well, I did anyway! I used to get undressed in the bathroom and dive into bed before Ray could see me – at one point I'd have rather died than walk round the bedroom naked when the lights were on.

Probably the only diet I haven't tried is the cabbage soup one, and my weight has yo-yoed ever since I became a mum. At my heaviest I was nearly fourteen stone and a size 20 – I remember going to a slimming club and being horrified when they weighed me. I was heavier than Ray and my sons! One day Ciara said to me, 'Mummy, you know when I was in your tummy and you were really fat? How come I'm out of your tummy and you're still really fat?' I laughed, but I realized she was right. There's nothing like being confronted by the cold hard truth to spur you into action. I lost three stone after that by following an extreme liquid diet, but as soon as I started eating proper food again, the weight piled back on.

I shaped up again for my wedding to Ray in 2007 – I was determined to walk down the aisle in a slinky wedding dress rather than a big meringue. This time I did it the healthy way, with a bit of help from slimming guru Rosemary Conley – not an opportunity most people get, I admit. I was offered the chance to make a fitness DVD with her about seven months before my big day and I followed her eating plan at the same time. I really wanted the DVD to do well and I didn't want to let anyone down – least of all myself – so it made me determined to shape up. And when I said 'I do' to Ray I was wearing the size 12 bodice dress I'd always dreamed of. It was such a confidence boost – I felt happier, sexier and had loads more energy. Ray was proud of me too, and even one of Shane Junior's friends said I looked 'hot'. I did a photoshoot wearing a red bikini and the picture was splashed all over the front page of the *Daily Mirror*! On my honeymoon in Cyprus I walked along the beach in my swimsuit without a sarong or shirt over the top. I hadn't done that in years.

## Back to Bad Habits

But gradually I fell back into my bad habits and the weight crept back on – nearly two stone of it! I used to moan to Ray, telling him I was getting fat again, while stuffing pizza in my mouth. He'd just look at me and say, 'Er . . . have you ever tried to stop eating that stuff?' He didn't have any time for my excuses and that's what they were.

Ray didn't care what size I was – he loved me regardless – but he knew being overweight made me miserable. I was sick of avoiding mirrors and wearing outsized frumpy clothes, and thinking I looked terrible all the time. I was determined to lose the weight again – and keep it off.

Dancing was my secret weapon – it doesn't feel like exercise to me at all, it feels like fun – so when I was asked to make another workout DVD (*Coleen Nolan's Disco Burn*) I didn't think twice. I'd also been asked to compete in *Dancing on Ice* and I didn't want to end up heaving myself around the rink like an elephant in a sparkly leotard! I wanted to give those young sexy female contestants a run for their money and prove that a forty-something mum of three could wear unforgiving Lycra costumes and look good. So I had a goal – and a time frame to get into shape. I believe having something to aim for – whether it's a family party, a reunion with old friends, a holiday or a wedding – is a great way to kick-start a weight-loss regime and keep you motivated.

The weight began to come off when I started training for the DVD and I changed my diet, too. It was nothing drastic – I just started eating more healthily. I made lots of little easy changes – I swapped full-fat milk for semi-skimmed, I used low-fat yoghurt in sauces instead of cream and, if I was hungry between meals, I had fruit instead of biscuits. It all added up.

I made sure I had three healthy meals every day so I wasn't tempted to snack on rubbish, and treats were just that – I had them now and again. Before I'd snack all day and think nothing of demolishing a packet of chocolate digestives with a cuppa.

You see, there is no 'miracle diet' – it doesn't exist! I know because I've done them all.

Weight loss isn't rocket science – you have to eat less of the bad stuff, eat more of the good stuff and move around more. That doesn't mean it's easy, particularly if you're a busy mum. But I found that once I'd started being more active and eating healthier foods, I didn't want to eat rubbish any more. You just need to break through the pain barrier until your healthier regime becomes part of your lifestyle. When you first notice you've lost a bit of weight, it really gives you confidence to keep going.

And don't beat yourself up if you have a bad day and give in to a biscuit binge. We've all been there, right? The important thing is to put it behind you and start afresh the next day.

## If I Can Do It, So Can You

It's a year since I appeared on *Dancing on Ice*, and I didn't look at all bad in those costumes (even if I say so myself!). And I did quite well, too, getting all the way to the semi-finals.

I've also managed to keep the weight off – I'm just under nine stone and a size 10–12. (I'll always be a size 12 on top because of my massive boobs – they're a 36GG!)

But after years of battling with my weight, I'm finally

happy with my body. And believe me, if I can do it, so can you. I'll never be a size zero – I'd look ridiculous anyway because of my humungous breasts! But I wouldn't want to be that skinny – it's much healthier and sexier to keep your womanly shape. I love being curvy.

Probably the best I've ever felt about my body was last year at the launch party for my autobiography *Upfront and Personal*. I arrived wearing a pair of skinny wet-look black leggings with a white tuxedo jacket and a pair of killer heels. I glided down the sweeping staircase of the swanky cocktail bar in central London with a gorgeous semi-naked male model on each arm (we're talking six packs to die for!). And it made me think about how far I'd come in my battle against the bulge. Those huge tent-like sequinned dresses I used to wear to parties and red-carpet events were definitely a thing of the past. I felt like a million dollars.

## My Three Golden Rules for . . . Diet Success

**Don't opt for faddy diets.** They don't work. I went on a liquid diet when I was at my heaviest and, although I lost three stone, I spent half my life on the toilet and as soon as I looked at a piece of toast, I piled the pounds back on.

**Choose an activity you love.** If you hate gyms, it's a waste of time forking out for an expensive membership because you won't go. You might as well chuck the money down the toilet. Do something you enjoy – take the buggy out to the park for a brisk walk or set aside some time to do a fitness DVD at home. Both options are a lot cheaper and more convenient, so you might actually have a chance of doing them.

**Don't deprive yourself of treats.** If you do this, it'll only make you miserable and you'll probably end up having a biscuit binge or just eating more of other things. I'm a total chocaholic, but now, instead of scoffing a whole bar, I'll just have a couple of squares. It's all about quantity.

## New Mums, Take Note!

You should wait six weeks after you've had your baby before thinking about doing any strenuous exercise or cutting back on food. If you've had a Caesarean, it's recommended you wait between six and eight weeks. Start with gentle exercise and build up slowly to more rigorous workouts. Your body has been through a lot, so take it easy! It's a good idea to check with your GP before starting any fitness regime after you've had a baby to make sure you're ready.

Breastfeeding can help you lose weight after the birth – although it doesn't work for everyone. Remember, though, you'll need about 500 calories more than usual each day to provide enough good milk for your baby – that means you should be consuming around 2,500 calories a day.

# Dance Your Way to a Slimmer You

Dancing round my living room to my *Disco Burn* DVD is what really kick-started my weight loss. A workout DVD is perfect for busy mums – you can do it when the baby's sleeping or your toddler is at nursery. And you don't have to worry about anyone else seeing you in a pair of Lycra leggings! Why not invite other mums over to join in and make it a social event, too? Ciara and her friends used to bring their cheerleading pom poms over to our house and dance along to my DVD with me – it was lots of fun. Here's why dancing can give you a better body:

- **It's a great aerobic workout.** It raises your heart rate and encourages your body to burn fat. Because it's fun, it doesn't feel like you're exercising. Going to a club or a salsa class with your friends for a night out is good exercise too – just don't mix it with too much alcohol!
- **You'll burn calories** – around 296 in an hour.
- **It strengthens your bones.** As a weight-bearing exercise, dancing wards off the bone-thinning disease osteoporosis.
- **It makes you fitter and stronger.** Regular dancing is great for improving endurance and overall fitness, so you'll find chasing after the kids or running for a bus that bit easier.

- **You'll tone up.** Dancing firms your muscles, making you look slimmer and leaner. It gives every bit of your body a workout, including your legs, bum and arms. Even your tummy will benefit as dancing requires good balance and that works your core muscles – far more fun than doing tons of sit-ups.

# My At Home Workout Tips

**Set the clock.** If time is an issue for you with the kids, try working out to your DVD first thing in the morning. I used to get up twenty or thirty minutes earlier to dance and, although the alarm was a challenge to begin with, once I'd done it a few times I found it really improved my mood for the rest of the day.

**Wear the right gear.** Some well-fitting trainers and a good bra are a must. If you're a big-busted woman like me, make sure you get fitted for a sports bra to avoid the bounce!

**Be consistent.** You'll only see the benefits if you keep it up – aim for twenty minutes, three times a week and gradually build up to an hour each time. There's no need to push yourself too hard to begin with.

**Warm up first.** This will prepare your body for exercise by gradually increasing your heart rate and body temperature and lubricating your joints. Stretching and jogging on the spot for a few minutes will do the trick.

**Cool it.** Be sure to wind down after dancing with some stretches. Good fitness DVDs include a warm-up and cool-down as part of the workout.

## More Easy Ways To Lose Your Mummy Tummy

**Walking.** It's the most convenient exercise there is. A twenty-minute walk at 3mph will burn about 80 calories. If you add a few hills, you'll burn as many calories as you would running.

We should take 10,000 steps a day (around five miles), but most of us only manage 3,000. There are sneaky ways of notching up those extra steps, though – walk about while you're on the phone and during ad breaks when you're watching telly, and always use the upstairs loo! If the school run is a five-minute drive, make it a fifteen-minute walk instead – fifteen minutes is better than nothing. You can keep track of how many steps you're taking with a pedometer, which you can buy cheaply from any sports shop. Taking the buggy out is a great way for new mums to get in plenty of walking – you can even join buggy fitness groups (try www.buggyfit.co.uk, which has classes nationwide).

**Swimming.** This is a great all-round exercise for burning calories and toning muscles, and it's a good stress reliever, too. You're supported by the water, so it doesn't put too much stress on your body, making it perfect for new mums. You'll burn around 272 calories if you swim for an hour at a moderate pace. If you've recently had a baby, don't swim until six weeks after the birth to avoid infection.

**Cycling.** Get on your bike instead of driving and you'll really burn those calories – 500 in an hour if you're going at a moderate pace. Cycling is great fun, too, and something the whole family can enjoy together.

**Yoga and Pilates.** Both of these are perfect for toning up saggy tummy muscles and they're great relaxation techniques, too. Just the thing after a stressful day with the kids! Visit www.yogapages.co.uk or www.pilatesfoundation.com to find a class in your area. Many studios and teachers offer post-natal classes for new mums. Go with a friend and make it a regular night out once a week.

# My Never-Be-Hungry Diet Plan

The key to sticking to healthy eating is to make sure you don't feel hungry all the time because you'll only end up snacking and ruining all your hard work. I hate feeling hungry – it's just miserable – so when I started my healthy diet plan, I made sure it was one that kept me feeling satisfied.

Try my meal plans to see if they work for you. If you're a vegetarian, opt for those dishes marked with a **V**. Vary your choices to make sure you get a variety of nutrients and have 300ml of semi-skimmed milk every day. Dairy products are packed with bone-building calcium. Eat lots of veg and salad – they're full of vitamins, minerals and fibre, but are low in calories and fat. And aim to drink between six and eight glasses of water daily, which will keep you hydrated and help fill you up, too.

### *Breakfast (200 calories)*

Choose one of the following each day:

- Two slices of wholemeal toast with low-fat spread and Marmite. **V**
- 4tbsp branflakes with semi-skimmed milk and one apple. **V**

- A bowl of fruit salad, one pot of fat-free fruit yoghurt, 2tbsp oats. V
- One slice of wholemeal toast with 4tbsp of baked beans. V
- Porridge: 3tbsp oats with 100ml water, 100ml milk and 1tbsp raisins. V
- One boiled egg with a slice of wholemeal toast and low-fat spread, and a handful of blueberries. V
- One bowl of instant oat cereal topped with raspberries. V

### *Snack (50 calories)*

Choose one of the following each day:

- Handful of grapes. V
- One apple. V
- One pot of fat-free fruit yoghurt. V
- 2tbsp reduced-fat tzatziki, one tomato, a small portion of cucumber. V
- One orange. V
- One slice of melon and a few raspberries. V
- One kiwi fruit and a satsuma. V

## *Lunch (300 calories)*

Choose one of the following each day:

- A medium-sized jacket potato, half a can of tuna in water, salad and fat-free dressing.
- A chicken salad sandwich made from two slices of wholemeal bread, low-fat spread, two slices of chicken breast and salad. Plus one apple.
- Half a carton of fresh bean soup and a wholemeal roll filled with a slice of lean ham and a sliced tomato. Plus a satsuma.
- A wholemeal pitta with half a tub of reduced-fat tzatziki and vegetable crudités. Plus one apple.
- A medium-sized jacket potato with 6tbsp fat-free cottage cheese and salad with fat-free dressing. **V**
- A cheese and tomato omelette made using spray oil, two eggs, a little milk, 4tbsp grated reduced-fat cheese and one tomato. Serve with salad. **V**
- One tortilla wrap filled with half a small avocado, a chopped tomato and some rocket. Plus one pot of fat-free fruit yoghurt. **V**

### *Snack (100 calories)*

Choose one of the following each day:

- A pear, a satsuma and a handful of raspberries. **V**
- Half a carton of vegetable soup. **V**
- One pot of fat-free yoghurt and a few strawberries. **V**
- One small packet of prawns with a salad.
- A banana. **V**
- 3tbsp reduced-fat hummus with carrot sticks. **V**
- Two rye crackers with 2tbsp low-fat soft cheese and a tomato. **V**

### *Evening Meal (400 calories)*

Choose one of the following each day:

- Cottage pie made with 100g extra-lean minced beef, one small onion, fat-free gravy, one small can of chopped tomatoes and one large potato mashed with semi-skimmed milk. Plus steamed veg to serve.
- One lean grilled pork chop with four new potatoes boiled in their skins and steamed veg. Plus an apple.
- Half a packet of stir-fry veg in half a jar of black bean sauce with 7tbsp of brown rice. Plus a satsuma. **V**
- Spaghetti Bolognese made from 100g extra-lean minced beef, a small onion, a carrot, a few mushrooms, one small can of chopped tomatoes, tomato purée, mixed herbs and fat-free

beef stock, with 130g of wholewheat spaghetti, salad and fat-free dressing.
- A 400-calorie (veggie or non-veggie) healthy-eating range ready-meal with salad or veg.
- Creamy mushroom pasta made using 8tbsp cooked wholewheat pasta, half a small packet of button mushrooms and one small onion fried in 1tsp olive oil, veg stock, a little white wine, a handful of spinach and 2tbsp reduced-fat crème fraîche. Top with 1tbsp Parmesan and serve with salad. **V**
- Roast chicken and Mediterranean vegetables: roast one skinless chicken breast with three new potatoes in their skins, half a red and half a green pepper, one courgette, a few cherry tomatoes and one small red onion in 2tsp olive oil.

### *Treat (100 calories)*

Choose one of the following each day
- Two Jaffa cakes or two small chocolate chip cookies. **V**
- A small pot of low-fat chocolate mousse. **V**
- A small glass of red or dry white wine. **V**
- A scoop of low-fat ice cream. **V**
- Five marshmallows. **V**
- Two single (25ml) measures of gin, vodka, rum or whisky with a diet mixer such as slimline tonic or diet cola. **V**
- One small packet of low-fat crisps. **V**

## Seven Diet Tips That Really Work

**Eat regular meals.** Skipping meals will only mean you'll end up snacking – usually on junk!

**Make little changes.** Small changes add up to make a big difference, so swap your usual full-fat products for low-fat versions. Use semi-skimmed or skimmed milk. If you like cheese, go for low-fat or reduced-fat versions or cottage cheese, which is naturally low in fat.

**Cook smart.** Grill, boil, poach, steam and roast without added fat or microwave food instead of frying it.

**Think lean.** Choose lean cuts of meat and skinless chicken and cut off fat before cooking.

**Fight the fat.** Eat fewer fatty meat products such as sausages, burgers, pies and pastry products.

**Junk the junk.** Cut back on high-fat treats like crisps, chocolate, cakes, pastries and biscuits.

**Leave the leftovers!** If you don't want to waste the food your kids leave, cover it and stick it in the fridge for lunch or a snack the next day.

FIVE

# School Days

# My Baby's Not a Baby Any More!

When Shane Junior started school his first day was the longest six hours of my life. I remember putting him in his uniform and thinking how little he looked. Far too little to go to school. As I left him in his classroom, smiling reassuringly and waving goodbye, he just looked up at me, his lip quivering, and I thought, 'Oh my God, what am I doing? I can't leave him here!'

I think that first day at school is just as hard for you as a mum as it is for your child. When Shane started school Jake was just a baby so he helped to keep me busy, but the house still seemed so quiet. I should have been looking forward to that bit of extra 'me time' I'd be getting now I wouldn't be running around after Shane – taking Jake in his pram to meet my friends for lunch, putting my feet up to watch a bit of daytime telly or having a nap while the baby slept. But I couldn't stop thinking about my little boy – all by himself in that big school.

On his first day I worried about him constantly, wondering if he was missing me, whether he'd made a little friend, if people were being kind to him. I couldn't wait to go and pick him up and give him a big hug. It was torture! I remember all my kids going through a stage when they first started school of coming home and saying they'd had a good day, then adding, 'But I'm not going back tomorrow.' It's not easy explaining to a four-year-old they have to go back every day till they're at least sixteen!

With all my kids, I found the best way of getting them used to the idea of starting school was to talk about it as though it wasn't a big deal, but still something to look forward to. I used to say things like, 'I can't believe what a big boy you are now. In fact, I think you're taller now you're going to school.' They love feeling special and grown-up. I also got them involved in choosing their uniforms and buying little pencil cases to help build the excitement.

The important thing to remember is that kids are very adaptable at this age and they will settle in eventually. Let's face it, it takes us a few months to get used to a new job or living in a new area, so it'll take them time, too. Ciara used to be very shy and when she started school she found all the new people and strange surroundings overwhelming, and she cried every day for two weeks! I had a word with her teacher, though, and things calmed down. Teachers in the reception years are used to this happening all the time and know how to deal with it. Now, of course, you can't shut Ciara up – school really helped her to come out of her shell.

But while you spend those first few weeks missing your 'baby' like crazy, as the months and years go by, you start to dread three o'clock coming round, when the kids come thundering through the door, chucking coats and shoes in the hall and filling your nice quiet house with noise and chaos! In the meantime, here are a few ideas to make those first days a little less stressful.

- **Get them to try on their new uniform.** My kids, especially Ciara, loved the idea of wearing a uniform. Getting them to try it on before the big day will help them get used to it.
- **Chat about school.** On the run-up to their first day, talk about the kinds of things they'll be doing at school and point the building out if you're driving or walking past. Talk through any fears they might have and reassure them. Explain to them about playtimes and lunchtime. And make sure you discuss all the fun activities they'll take part in, too, such as painting and games.
- **Team up with friends.** If your child has been to nursery, they might know some of the kids who'll be in their class. Team up with some of the other mums and arrange a play-date where you can talk about them all going to school together.
- **Sort out the practicalities.** Remember to put name tags on absolutely everything you can – from PE kits to lunchboxes. Visit www.nametag-it.co.uk, which has personalized iron-on, sew-on and stick-on labels. And put a calendar up

in the kitchen so you can keep track of school holidays, trips, events, parents' evenings and invites.

- **Get involved with other mums and dads.** Becoming friendly with parents at the school gates can help your kids make friends. You could get a whole new social life out of it, too!

# What They Should Know Before They Start School

There's a lot of nonsense talked about how much your kids should know before they go to school. At four or five they're probably already anxious about starting school, so they don't need any extra pressure. Plus they have years and years of learning ahead of them, so give them a break! If they don't know the alphabet and can't count to fifty, that's perfectly okay – that's what they're going to school for.

Teachers are trained to build on what each child knows and compensate for what they don't. But there are some basic skills they should have got to grips with, which will help them cope better at school. They should be able to:

- Tell you their full name and address.
- Dress themselves, do up zips and tie shoelaces.
- Use a knife and fork.
- Go to the toilet by themselves.
- Tidy up their toys.
- Take turns and share with other children.
- Sing simple songs.

# Help! My Son Hates His New School

**My six-year-old son has just started a new school and he hates it. He loved his last school and he misses his friends. What can I do to help him?**

Teachers are very good at coping with situations like this. I'd have a word with the staff at your son's new school and explain that he's finding it hard to adjust. Ask them to keep an eye on him to make sure he's OK.

Your son is still young, though, and although he misses his old school at the moment, children of his age are very good at adapting to new situations. Some may take longer than others, but I'm sure within a few weeks he'll be fine. You can do things to help him make friends more easily. Find out who his favourite person in the class is and then invite them round for a play-date. You could also organize a tea party with some children from his class or take them all out for a burger. Get him involved in any after-school activities and clubs where he can make friends in a more relaxed and fun environment.

Obviously, as a mum you feel guilty at upsetting your son's routine, but a word of warning – don't let him play on your guilt. Kids are good at that!

## My Three Ways To . . .
## Make the School Run Easier

**Lay out their things the night before.** I find it's much easier to get organized at night when you have more time. Lay out their clothes, PE kits and school books ready for the morning. It's not a bad idea to lay your things out, too!

**Start a little earlier.** We all know a lie-in is a rare luxury, so try getting everyone up fifteen minutes earlier so you're not rushing around in a blind panic. And ensure the kids have a strict morning routine where they do things in the same order – it makes everything run more smoothly.

**Get the older children to help.** If you have kids of varying ages, ask the elder ones to help with the younger children. Shane Junior and Jake were very good at helping Ciara with her breakfast. By helping out they can earn privileges like extra pocket money.

# Help! My Five-Year-Old Is a Fussy Eater

**My five-year-old daughter turns her nose up at practically everything I give her to eat. The only foods she actually eats without a fuss are mashed potato and bread! How can I encourage her to eat other things?**

Well, if it's any consolation, I live with 'Miss I Won't Eat Anything apart from Chicken Nuggets and Rice'. Actually, I'm being a bit hard on Ciara, she also eats spaghetti Bolognese occasionally! But she won't touch fruit or veg.

All my kids were fussy eaters – Shane ate nothing but mashed potatoes and beans till he was about twelve and Jake would only eat meat and potatoes. I was always taking both boys to the doctor, worried about their nutrition, but they always got a clean bill of health. Now of course, they'll eat anything.

I still have a battle on my hands with Ciara but I'm hoping she'll grow out of it like the boys. I've tried everything with her – from cutting veg into interesting shapes to hiding it in mashed potato and telling her I've put magic colours in there! She doesn't buy it.

Some experts say if kids don't eat what's in front of them then don't offer any other options, so they'll have to eat it. In reality, it's hard to stick to this when your child is crying about being hungry. You could also try getting your daughter involved in helping to make the meal so it's fun and she wants to eat it. The most effective tactic I've tried with Ciara is to cut down on snacks during the day so she's ready for her tea. I would also recommend you persevere with offering your daughter a wide variety of foods, but keep the portions small so it's not overwhelming. I keep giving Ciara fruit and veg because I'm convinced that one day she'll turn round and accept it.

It's easy to feel guilty about what you do or don't feed your kids these days because we're constantly bombarded with information on what's good and bad for them and that advice seems to change on a weekly basis. If your daughter is healthy, happy and active, I don't think you have too much to worry about.

## My Three Ways To . . .
## Get Them to Eat Veg

**Don't get angry.** I have found encouragement works better with Ciara than getting annoyed. It's no good telling them, 'Children are dying in poor countries,' as they'll inevitably reply, 'Well, send them my dinner then!'

**Don't overload them.** They'll be more likely to give new foods a go if you start them off with small portions.

**Put the fun back.** Say, 'OK, I'll try it too!' and give them loads of praise. After they've tried a fingerful of something, say: 'I'm sure you're getting taller!' which will excite them.

# Pack a Healthy Lunch

Kids need a good lunch to keep them going at school. They'll want crisps and chocolate biscuits in their lunchbox, but here are some healthy options that'll boost their brainpower and their energy levels, too.

- Use wholemeal bread or rolls instead of white, as it contains more fibre.
- Fill their sandwiches with lean meat like chicken or turkey. Tinned tuna (in water), a thin slice of cheese or sliced banana are also good options. And don't go overboard on the butter and mayo.
- Always give them fruit. If they're bored with apples and bananas, fill a small tub with grapes or berries, which are easier to eat. Kids like those little boxes of raisins, too.
- Include some easy-to-eat raw veg like cherry tomatoes or carrot, pepper and cucumber sticks.
- Instead of fizzy drinks, which are packed with sugar and chemical additives, give them some diluted fruit juice. Flavoured milkshakes are a good source of calcium but shop-bought ones can contain a lot of sugar. Make your own shakes with semi-skimmed milk (for over-fives) with a little milkshake syrup to control how much sugar they have.

## *My Three Ways to . . .*
## *Improve Their Table Manners*

**Lead by example.** Start by setting your own standards. If you have good manners then they'll pick up from your example. So make sure you're not talking with your mouth full and that you hold your knife properly. They'll follow your lead.

**Get them to say please.** Teaching them to say please and thank you is a major thing. Good behaviour at meal times all starts from having a clear routine. Once their food is in front of them they should know to say thank you.

**Make it fun.** Meals can seem boring if they're out playing and having fun when you call them to the table. I know I used to hate dinner time as a kid. So use the time to talk and laugh with them and find out about their day. If they don't feel it's a chore, they'll be better behaved.

## A Word About Allergies

When I was growing up none of my friends had allergies, but these days it seems children are allergic to everything – from everyday foods such as milk, eggs and nuts to dust mites and honey. Yet another thing for mums to worry about! I was lucky enough that none of my lot had any serious allergies, but if you think your child might be allergic to something, see your GP. You can also visit www.blossomcampaign.org for lots of helpful information on childhood allergies.

## I'm Leaving Him for the First Time

**I'm going away on a week-long course for work, but I've never left my five-year-old before. His dad is taking time off work to be with him and we've also arranged a childminder, but my son is quite clingy. How can I prepare him for me being away?**

This will be hard for you, but if your son is clingy, it could be a good thing for him. You have to go away and, after all, it is only for a few days. I can guarantee if he's sobbing his heart out when you go, the minute the door closes he will stop. I remember having to leave my boys for a while when they were young and they were so upset I had to peel them off my legs. But of course as soon as I left they were absolutely fine. I would explain to your son in advance that you're going away for work. Reassure him that you'll be back soon and that he'll have a great time with Daddy. And tell him, 'If you're a good boy then you'll get a present when I come back.' It doesn't have to be a big thing. OK, it's bribery, but it works, and it will make you both feel better.

The truth is, going away usually ends up being much harder for the parent than the child. You'll miss him so much and feel guilty every day you're away, but the time will whizz by and you'll be back before you know it.

## My Three Ways To . . . Get Them to Bed on Time

**It's all about preparation.** Set a realistic time frame for your kids when they're getting ready for bed. There's no point giving them ten minutes to get settled before lights out – but you don't want them to drag out the proceedings either.

**Establish a bedtime routine.** Start your preparations at the same time every night, say with a bath at seven, then a snack, before tucking them into bed for a story by a quarter to eight. That way they'll be ready for lights out at 8 p.m.

**Stay calm and keep your cool.** The minute you get stressed they'll start stressing too, and it will take twice as long for them to be ready for sleep.

# My Son Is Rude to Visitors

**My five-year-old son is very rude if we have guests. He won't speak or answer questions and is sullen – it's embarrassing! Is there anything I can do?**

You probably feel your son's behaviour reflects badly on you, but it doesn't – all children go through funny stages. The thing is to ignore him and not let it become an issue. Explain to your guests that he's not in a very talkative mood and just get on with entertaining them. I have no doubt he's probably behaving like this to seek attention. He knows if he's sullen and difficult then he'll get attention from you – even if it's negative – so don't give it to him. Eventually, he won't like being ignored and will come round. Tell him quietly that when he can talk nicely he can join in. I think you'll find he'll soon get bored of his behaviour and make more effort.

# He's Scared to Sleep Over

**My five-year-old son won't stay at his friends' houses for sleepovers. He's happy to have pals here, but when he's at a friend's party we always have to pick him up at 8.30 p.m. because he says he's scared. Is there anything I can do to encourage him?**

I had the same thing with Shane Junior, but Jake stayed over at his friends' homes from the age of four! Ciara on the other hand has only just started to have sleepovers and she's eight. There is no set rule. Each child is different and if your son doesn't like to stay over then that's OK, and you shouldn't worry. Of course, you can reassure him that there's no reason to be scared, but perhaps he's worried that if he wakes up during the night he won't know who to turn to for comfort. Some kids just like the security of their own home and bed, and you can't push them into staying with a friend if they don't want to.

Your son is still only five and probably just needs a bit more time before he's ready – he might be ten or eleven before he feels comfortable with it. The good thing is, he's still going to parties and interacting with other children, so don't be worried that he has social issues. In my book, picking him up at 8.30 p.m. is better than getting a frantic phone call to come and get him at 3 a.m.!

## My Three Ways To . . . Encourage Kids to Read and Play On Their Own

**Start them off.** It's essential that children get plenty of attention, but also that they learn to entertain themselves. It can be hard to get them to sit down and focus, so give them a drink or a biscuit and start them off, then leave them to it.

**Give them praise.** Tell them they don't need you to hold their hand every time. Say, 'You're getting so big now, you can play on your own.' Your child will love the praise.

**Reward them with your time.** Tell them that if they're good and can amuse themselves for the moment, then you'll promise to come and play with them half an hour later.

# *My Son Is Obsessed By Women's Breasts*

**Don't laugh, but my five-year-old has developed an unhealthy obsession with women's breasts. He touches my friends' boobs all the time. What can I do to stop him?**

You son is five and very curious, that's all. I don't think you need to worry that he's a sex-mad pervert just yet! If you turn it into a big deal, you'll only make it worse. And if you laugh, he'll think it's a joke and do it again for attention. But if you tell him off then he'll think what he's doing is wrong – and it's not. If I were you I would just try to change the subject. So say, 'Yes, yes, they're breasts, now how about doing some colouring?' If he has any questions, simply answer them and then move on.

To make you feel less anxious, why not warn your friends before they come round. Say, 'My son has a mad obsession with breasts at the moment, so don't be worried if he tries to touch yours.' I'm sure they'll just think it's funny. Kids of this age are also naturally curious about bodies. My two boys were and Ciara was always asking why women's bodies are different from men's, and when she was going to get boobs!

Your son will be obsessed with them for a bit, then he'll go off them and think, 'Ugh, girls, yuck!' Then he'll get obsessed again when he hits puberty. It's absolutely fine for him to behave like this at five – if he's doing it at fifteen, that's when you need to worry!

♥

## Is Seven Too Young for a Mobile Phone?

**My seven-year-old wants a mobile phone. Part of me feels I should give her one so she can contact me in an emergency, but is she too young?**

Yes, she is far too young! She probably wants one because some of her friends have a mobile. I've had exactly the same problem with Ciara recently – a lot of her friends who are seven and eight have mobiles, but I refuse to give in and get her one. At seven there shouldn't be any times when you don't know where daughter is. And, if you need to contact her at school, then you can call the teachers. After all, kids aren't allowed to use their mobiles at school.

My two boys were both twelve when they got mobile phones. At that age they're spending more time alone – walking home from school and visiting friends. I understand that as a mum you always want to be able to get in touch with your child, but if your child doesn't want you to contact them, all they have to do is not pick up!

I don't think it's right for seven-year-olds to be spending lots of time texting and calling each other on mobiles. I'd much rather Ciara was reading or playing creatively or running round with her friends outside. That's what kids should be doing.

Plus, mobiles are so expensive. At one point my boys were costing me £50 a week in phone credit. When they got older I made them pay for their own phones out of their allowance and suddenly they started using them less. Funny that!

I would wait until your daughter is twelve before considering buying her a phone.

## My Three Ways To . . .
## Keep Them Happy On a Car Journey

**Play 'I Spy'.** Ciara loves playing this. It keeps her happy for ages (although I get a bit bored!). You could also try car-journey alphabet – give them some paper and a pencil and get them to spot something on the journey for each letter of the alphabet.

**Schedule regular stops.** It's unrealistic to expect children to cope with a really long car journey without a break. Make sure you stop regularly for half an hour. It will give them a chance to run around and get rid of some pent-up energy.

**Try a portable DVD player.** You can buy these pretty cheaply now and they're a great investment for long journeys. Pop on their favourite film and they'll be amused for at least an hour. Or give them your MP3 player with their music on it.

# She Stole From Her Friend

**A few weeks ago my seven-year-old daughter came home with a new necklace. She told me her friend gave it to her, but I've since found out that her friend has been in tears because she can't find it. How should I handle this?**

The worst thing you can do is say nothing. If you ignore it then your daughter will think she's got away with it and that she can do it again whenever she sees something else she likes. She's only seven, so it doesn't mean she's going to commit the next Great Train Robbery, but you need to nip it in the bud before it becomes a habit. It's a big learning curve for her. It's clear she's just seen something she liked and chanced it – and hoped no one would find out.

Don't get angry with her – sit her down and explain what she's done wrong and tell her firmly, 'You don't steal from people.' To teach her a lesson, take her to her friend to give the necklace back in person. It's a mistake most of us have made as children and I'm sure her friend's mum will understand and appreciate you trying to make things right. After I nicked chewing gum from a sweet-shop when I was seven, I went to bed terrified the police would come and arrest me, and I never did it again! As long as you put a stop to it now, and make it clear to her that it's not acceptable behaviour, she ought to get the message.

# He's Still Wetting the Bed At Seven

**My seven-year-old son keeps wetting the bed. It makes him feel anxious and embarrassed and I don't know how to help him. Have you got any advice?**

The main thing is to keep calm. The more anxious you get, the more nervous he'll become. What you don't want is for him to get so embarrassed that he feels he has to hide it from you.

There are lots of reasons why he may be wetting the bed. He could be a really deep sleeper and doesn't wake up when he needs the loo. It could be as simple as changing his routine so he gets out of the habit.

One idea is to put him to bed and, then, when you go to bed later at, say, midnight, wake him up and take him to the toilet. Kids normally don't wake up properly so it won't disturb him too much, but it will help him stop wetting the bed. You should also stop him drinking anything two hours before bedtime and make sure he goes to the loo before going to sleep.

If he's wetting the bed regularly, your GP can prescribe an alarm with a moisture-sensitive pad that'll wake him up when he starts to wee, and then you can take him to the toilet. It's not a bad idea to talk to your GP anyway, because occasionally bed-wetting can be a sign of a health problem such as diabetes or a bladder infection.

If your son has suddenly started wetting the bed after being dry at night, it could be because there's something worrying him. For example, it could be sign he's being bullied or that he's unhappy at school. Talk to him about his friends and how he's enjoying school to see if it throws up any clues, and maybe have a word with his teacher.

However, more often than not, the problem just goes away on its own. My friend's son was bed-wetting right up to the age of eight, but for him it was just a case of being too lazy to get up! It used to drive my friend mad, but he grew out of it.

## My Three Ways To . . . Stop Siblings Squabbling

**Find out the reason.** It's often because of a toy they both want. Separate them and take the toy away, then split the time so they can each have it for twenty minutes. It'll teach them a valuable lesson about sharing.

**Get them to sort it out.** An age gap with siblings can cause problems. The younger one often idolizes the older child and wants to be with them, but the older one doesn't want to play with the 'baby'! Sit them both down and find out the problem. Then get them to find ways of solving it themselves – it'll make them feel more grown-up.

**Keep cool – it's natural!** You can't stop every sibling row – for kids it's a big part of growing up and finding out who they are. It's all about teaching them to listen to each other and helping them realize there's no point arguing. But to get to that stage there will be lots of rows along the way. Try to keep calm and help defuse the situation.

**AVOIDING INJURIES**

Little ones are at risk of getting hurt when a spat erupts and fists start flying. I had a firm 'No hitting' rule with both Shane and Jake, so as soon as things got violent they'd be sent to separate rooms for a time out. I also explained to Shane that he was older and stronger and that if he hit Jake back he could really hurt him. Whenever Shane managed to keep his cool, I made sure I gave him lots of praise, which made him feel grown-up and special.

## Her Kids Are Out of Control

**My friend has boys aged four, six and eight and they are the most disobedient children I've ever met. Whenever they visit they wreck our house and neither parent seems to be able to control them. How do I broach the subject without offending them? At the moment, I'm avoiding contact with them, as I don't want them visiting.**

You must deal with this situation very carefully because their mother's instinct will be to stand up for her kids if you say anything negative about them. There's a good chance you'll fall out if you criticize the children – I know people who have fallen out over a situation like this.

The trick is to invite her round when the kids aren't there or suggest you both get a babysitter and have a girls' night out. If it really is impossible to see her without her boys, then why not suggest meeting up in a park or at the beach. The boys can play nearby while you both catch up. If she asks why you haven't been in touch, then you'll have to be very tactful in your reply. Don't say, 'They're little horrors who wreck my house.' Try to be light-hearted and perhaps say something like, 'The boys are wild and it's tiring being around them.' It's hard to know how she'll respond. It would take a big woman to turn around and say, 'Yes, they are a nightmare.' Alternatively, you could try to coax her into talking about the kids and if she agrees they are difficult to control, you can offer her some suggestions.

It is a frustrating situation – I've had kids come round to mine and go crazy, and you can't understand why their parents just sit there and don't say anything. I'd never let my kids behave badly in someone else's house. At the end of the day, if they're in your house and ruining your things, you have every right to tell them to stop. Hopefully, they will hate being at your place so much they'll say, 'I don't want to go round to her house – she's too strict,' and all your problems will be solved!

## How to Tackle Lying

I hate lying and my kids know it's the one thing I won't tolerate. It's probably got something to do with what happened in my marriage – I had many months of my ex-husband Shane lying to me while he was having an affair. So I've always been tough on my kids when it comes to lies.

The way I handled it was to tell them never to lie to me because if they got found out the consequences would be so much worse than if they'd told me the truth! You have to be true to your word, though, so when they do confess to something bad like flushing your purse down the toilet or breaking your favourite vase, you have to react in a way that doesn't make them think, 'Next time I won't tell the truth because she'll go mental!'

You have to let them know you're not happy but that you appreciate them being honest. I remember Jake smashed up his first mobile phone in a temper tantrum and told me it had fallen out of his pocket and been run over by a truck. He handed me this phone that was in a million pieces and it was clear it hadn't been run over by anything, so I asked him to tell me the truth. He owned up to smashing it against the wall. I think he thought I'd buy him a new phone, but I didn't – he had to save up for one himself. He learnt his lesson.

## Should I Get Him a Pet Rabbit?

**My son is desperate to get a pet rabbit but we live in a flat so it's impossible. I hate saying no to him, but I don't have any option. How can I let him down gently?**

Well, you're wrong, actually. It is possible to have a pet rabbit indoors – I know this because we have one. We have a house bunny called Holly and she mainly stays indoors. She lives in a big hutch in the house and we open the door and she jumps in and out. She's very cute and friendly – we've got two dogs but she gets on with them fine. In fact, she actually chases them around. You can even house-train rabbits if they stay indoors. I personally believe it's a good thing for kids to grow up with some kind of animal. I think having a pet teaches them about kindness and gentleness.

I've noticed with Ciara's friends that there's a big difference between the ones who have pets at home and those who don't. The friends who don't have pets tease our dogs but the ones who do stroke them and show an immediate kindness towards them. I also think having a pet gives children a sense of responsibility. Ciara helps to clean out the hutch – I do the dirty bit but she lays down the fresh straw and sawdust. On top of this she also gives Holly her food and water. It's nice for Ciara because it's her little job and she takes pride in caring for her. All in all it's a good lesson in life.

## He Swore At the Dinner Table

**My four-year-old was making a scene about finishing his vegetables during a family dinner and suddenly shouted: 'This food is s**t.' I've never heard him swear before, but my horrified mother-in-law now thinks I'm a bad mum. How can I stop him being rude again?**

You can't! As soon as you pull him up on it, he'll know it winds you up and he'll use it against you. From then on, if he's having a tantrum he'll know he can swear to get attention.

Your son is at an age when he will parrot things. He's obviously heard that word somewhere – from an older sibling or even his dad – and thought he'd try it out to see how it sounds. I think you should ignore it. If he keeps doing it, though, say something like, 'Only really horrible boys say things like that, and you won't have any friends.'

As for your mother-in-law, don't worry. I bet she went through something similar with her own precious son!

♥

## *How Can I Make Him More Outgoing?*

**My six-year-old is very shy and tends to prefer his own company to mixing in a large group. He's very happy being independent, but I'm worried he doesn't make friends easily. How can I make him more sociable?**

My sister Maureen's son, Danny, was the same. He was really unsociable and used to say to people when they came round, 'I hate you, get out of my house!' And he didn't like being with other kids. When he started going to school, Maureen actually hid behind the car to watch him and he'd be standing on his own in the playground. Maureen used to really worry about it because, out of all of us sisters, she loves being with people the most. She actually used to force Danny to give birthday parties that he didn't even want!

But now Danny is grown-up, he's really sociable and friendly, so just because your son is unsociable now doesn't mean he will be when he's older. I'm wondering if your son is an only child, because this is quite common in kids without brothers or sisters. Danny was an only child and enjoyed having his mum's full attention.

So don't worry. If I were you I'd still arrange social events so he gets used to having people around him – he doesn't need to talk to them! School will help him, too. Making friends will get easier and he'll gradually come out of himself. It might be an idea to speak to his teacher so she can keep an eye on him and help him integrate with the other kids. You could also try to get him interested in an after-school activity like swimming to help him meet other children.

# Make Friends, Never, Ever Break Friends!

Some kids are better than others at making friends. For some, mixing with all those new kids at school is exciting, but for others it's daunting. There are things you can do, however, to help them along when it comes to making friends. Here's how . . .

- **Invite other kids round.** Ciara was very shy when she started school, so to combat this I'd let her bring a friend over for tea. It really helped for her to have the security of her own environment and she became more confident. Organize play-dates with other mums where you take turns in having their kids over or take them to the park or to see a movie. Look into after-school clubs – it's all about giving them opportunities.
- **Don't force *your* personality on them!** You might be the sort of person who's always first on the dance floor at a wedding, but don't expect your kids to have inherited your party gene. They might be naturally more reserved and that's OK.
- **Give them a chance to warm up.** Some kids are shy when they meet new people. Ciara can be like this, but she comes

out of her shell when she gets to know them better. Don't try to force them to make friends – allow them some time and space to do it their way.

- **Introduce them to people.** Children who are used to social situations tend to find it easier to make friends. My boys always had lots of different faces around when they were young and were used to mixing with adults. This made them more confident when it came to interacting with new children and developing friendships.
- **Improve their social skills.** Talk to them about the importance of listening to other people's points of view, how to ask questions, what it takes to be a good friend and how to treat people kindly.
- **Be a good listener.** Encourage them to talk about their friends at school and what happens at playtime. Talk about making new friends as an exciting and fun thing to do.
- **Watch out for trouble.** If you think your child is being picked on or teased at school, nip it in the bud by talking to their teacher as soon as possible. Signs to look out for are not wanting to go to school, wetting the bed and a change in mood. For more on this, see Beating the Bullies on page 215.

SIX

# My Summer Holiday Survival Guide

# All Together Now . . . 'I'm Bored!'

During the school holidays, Shane Junior and Jake would spring out of bed, wash and dress, eat a healthy breakfast without moaning, then head off to the garden to amuse themselves for the rest of the day.

Er . . . I wish! In reality, they'd mope about the house whining, 'Mum, I'm bored,' every five seconds, or they'd be screaming blue murder at each other. I could never decide which was worse. And that was if I could actually haul them out of bed before midday.

There's no doubt those six weeks can seem like a life sentence for mums, especially if the weather's rotten. So I've come up with a few ideas, with a bit of help from the mums I know, to keep your little angels busy (and stop you going nuts!).

# My Twenty-One Ways to Have a Happy Holiday

1. **Get arty.** The beauty of summer weather is that the kids can get as messy as they want outside and you don't have to worry about your carpet getting ruined. Set them up with paint and large pieces of paper in the back garden and get them to make paintings with handprints and footprints. You can always hose them down afterwards or pop them in the paddling pool!
2. **Have a tea party.** Get them to help you bake some easy fairy cakes and biscuits in the morning, then have a little afternoon tea party in the back garden and invite a couple of their friends.
3. **Improve their writing skills.** If it's raining outside, get them to write letters to friends and family and take them to the postbox afterwards. Ciara loves writing in her diary, so why not buy them a little book and get them to keep a journal of all the things they did on their summer holiday.
4. **Have a mini sports day.** Ask them to invite a few of their friends over and award little prizes for skipping, running

and egg and spoon races. They'll have fun and burn tons of excess energy!

5. **Don't save board games for Christmas.** Another good idea for a rainy day is a board-game tournament. Get them playing snakes and ladders or Operation.
6. **Go to the movies (at home).** You can pick up classic films on DVD from as little as £3, so invest in a few or rent some from your local video store. Then buy some treats like popcorn, hot dogs and tortilla chips, dim the lights and let them have a movie night with their friends.
7. **Reward them for decluttering their rooms.** Give older kids an incentive to sort out their bedrooms by booking a car-boot pitch, so they can sell their old toys, clothes and games. Let them keep the profits to spend on what they want – as long as they put in the work! Visit www.carbootjunction.com to find car-boot sales in your area.
8. **Have a pool party.** When the sun comes out, get a small paddling pool, a few deckchairs and a bat and ball game. Make some home-made fruit ice-lollies and fruit-juice cocktails and let them go nuts!
9. **Create a teen den.** Teenagers spend most of their lives in their bedrooms, so why not channel some of their creativity into sprucing it up? Let them mock up a theme, then buy some paint and get them to do the decorating. Buy some cheap, funky furniture in second-hand shops or car-boot

sales. They could also turn their favourite photos into cushions, mugs or posters – visit www.photobox.co.uk. Maybe once they've created their perfect bedroom, they'll keep it a bit tidier!

10. **Put on a show.** Get little ones to perform a show for you based on a theme – it could be something from a nursery rhyme or a favourite story. Put a sheet over the washing line to use as a curtain and have some little snacks for the interval. Older kids could make their own movie with a digital camera and you can all sit down for a viewing in the evening.
11. **Get them to love sport.** This is the perfect time to get them involved in healthy activities, which hopefully they'll grow to love. Visit www.direct.gov.uk and type in your postcode – it'll find all the sports facilities in your area from tennis courts and swimming pools to ice rinks and ski slopes!
12. **Visit museums and galleries.** This might sound dull, but once they see a dinosaur skeleton or a World War II bomber, they'll be hooked! Many museums are free of charge and hold special workshops and events for kids over the holidays. Visit www.culture24.org.uk to find out what's going on.
13. **Become farmers for the day!** Most children love young animals – I know Ciara is mad about them – so take them to visit a city farm. They can often feed and play with lambs or piglets, and learn about farming and growing food.

Make sure they wash their hands after petting the animals! Visit www.farmgarden.org.uk to find one near you.

14. **Be king and queen of the castle.** Many historic buildings such as castles and stately homes run events during the summer. Visit www.english-heritage.org.uk, www.historic-scotland.gov.uk, www.heritageireland.ie, www.national-trust.org.uk for ideas.
15. **Volunteer!** Teens over sixteen can get work experience over the holidays by signing up to V, the youth volunteering charity in England. It can match your teen to local projects that interest them. Visit www.vinspired.com.
16. **Get them into garden games.** These days all mums are battling the curse of computer games, but summer is the perfect time to encourage children to spend time away from the screen with backyard activities like badminton, cricket, bowling and croquet – and you can join in the fun, too.
17. **Holiday at home.** If you're having a staycation this summer, you can still bring a bit of foreign fun home. Pick a country as your theme and get the kids lost in a different culture for the day – if it's Spain, for example, buy a few cheap sombreros, put on some flamenco music and have tapas for dinner. If it's the States, put on a Beach Boys CD, dress the kids like surfer dudes and stick some burgers and hot dogs on the barbecue. You get the picture!
18. **Get busy in the backyard.** Create a little area in the garden where the kids can grow seeds or cuttings. Or get them to

plant flowers in pots they've painted themselves. They'll love watering them and watching them grow.

19. **Turn them into happy campers.** If you want to keep them entertained for a whole working week, try Do It 4 Real summer camps. They cater for children aged between ten and nineteen, and offer activities such as the performing arts, film and media, action adventure and survival skills. Visit www.doit4real.co.uk. PGL Holidays (www.pgl.co.uk) has been running adventure packages for kids for half a century and takes children as young as seven. It also has two-night breaks and 'first-timer' holidays where all the kids are newcomers.
20. **Let them have a grown-up party.** If you have tweens or teens, why not say they can host a small party in the garden with a few mates? Agree on the music level and a time to wrap things up, and supervise from a distance – remember children this age don't want their uncool mums hanging around!
21. **Pitch a tent.** Let older kids and teens have a sleepover with a difference by pitching a tent in the back garden. If you don't want them out there all night, bring them in at bedtime. Provide a torch, mugs of hot chocolate and enough marshmallows to keep them going for a while!

*Left* I remember thinking this outfit was cute. Why did no one tell me it wasn't, even for a pregnant woman?!

*Below Right* Shane always had the cutest smile. (When he wasn't screaming that is.)

*Bottom* Jake's favourite bathroom was the kitchen sink!

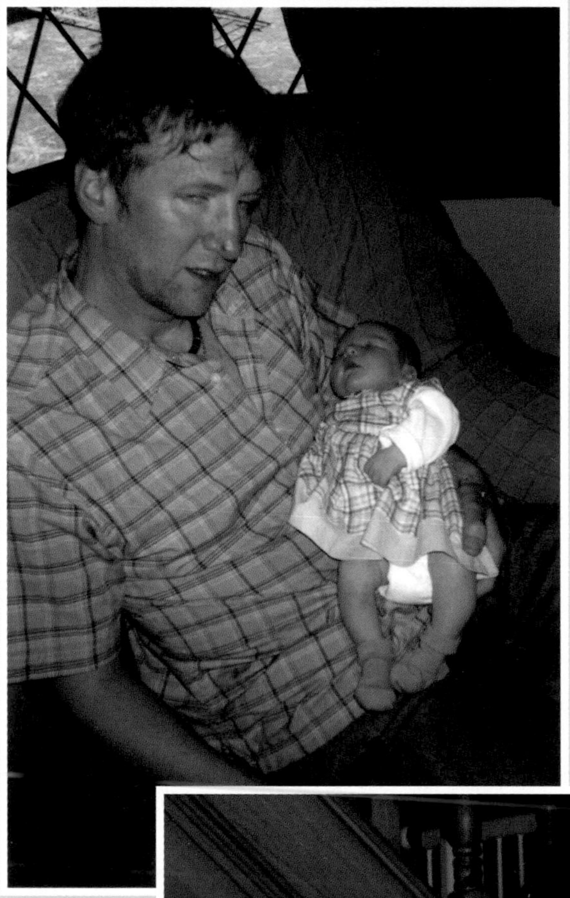

*Left* Ray and his new baby girl looking exhausted and half dead!

*Below* Ciara aged two trying out her hairdressing skills.

Jake aged eighteen months. It didn't matter how he ate, as long as he ate! (I'm sure some of it reached his stomach!)

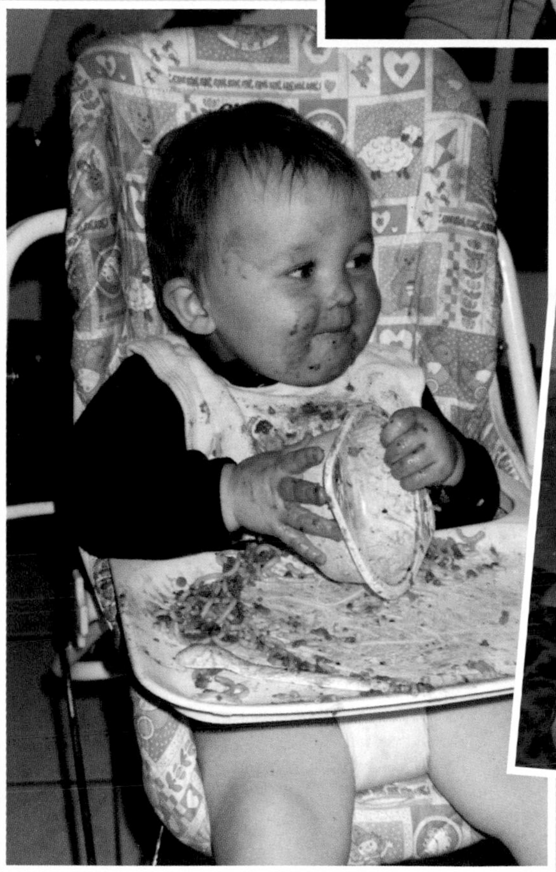

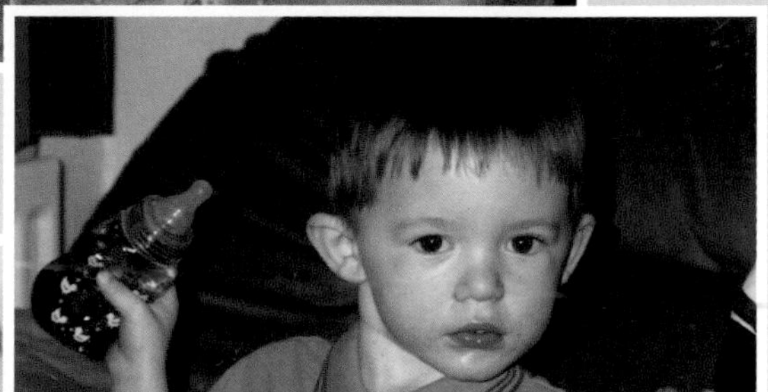

*Above left* Ciara aged twenty months letting me know the party is over.

*Above right* A bottle and a dummy? Anything to keep him quiet!

*Left* Did I mention Shane's terrible two stage? You have no idea how loud that scream was!

There were times when
they truly loved each other.
Not many though!

*Left* Photos are such fabulous memories as they grow up so fast.

*Below left* Jake at eighteen months. I think I was ready to post him at this stage!

*Bottom left* I don't know who was more thrilled when Shane learned to ride a bike!

*Below right* It only takes a moment like this to forgive them everything.

*Left* Wouldn't be the last time these two ended up in Mum's court!

*Below* Happy families! I love the times we all get to be together.

My rabble in 2009, all grown up. Being a mum is the best job in the world!

## STAY COOL WHEN TEMPERATURES RISE!

It wouldn't be the school holidays if the kids didn't fight among themselves or wind you up because they're bored. So when I'm on the verge of losing my temper, I always go into another room to regain my composure. Usually, I'll say: 'I'm going to walk out of the room now to calm down and I'd like you to leave me alone for a while.' Then, later, I'll talk to them calmly about their bad behaviour.

## LET THEM AMUSE THEMSELVES!

Remember, children don't need structured play or activities all the time. It's important to give them space to let their imaginations run wild and play make-believe, climb trees and make dens (just wrestle that computer game out of their mitts first!).

# What If You're a Working Mum?

The school holidays can be tough for mums who work. Even if you take a fortnight off for your summer break, you still have four weeks of childcare to organize. I was lucky – when my boys were at school, I was able to rely on relatives to take them during the holidays. Now we have Ciara, Ray and I share the childcare, depending on who's working at the time. However, it's a different story if you don't have family nearby who are willing to help or if you don't have the possibility of flexible working.

Some nurseries will take children up to the age of eight during the school holidays, but this is usually a pricey option. Why not visit your local authority website to find out about affordable holiday playschemes? Your local church and community centre may also offer holiday schemes for school-age kids, which can be half the price of a private nursery.

For older kids and teens, there's always the option of a residential summer camp (see point 19 above). This may only solve your problem for a week – but it's still a week of childcare sorted! You'll have the peace of mind that they're in a safe and stimulating environment, and they'll have fun and enjoy a bit of independence.

# She Won't Come On Holiday With Us

**My husband and I have booked a week off for a family holiday, but my sixteen-year-old daughter is refusing to come with us. She says that she'd rather hang out with her friends, as it will be boring with us. I want us to spend some proper time together but I also don't want to force her. What should I do?**

I don't think she should have the option to stay at home – tell her you'll understand if at eighteen she doesn't want to come with you. But explain that now you want to spend time with her. Make her feel wanted and tell her it's only one week out of her life. Also explain that it won't be boring, because you'll find things for her to do.

She's just trying to spread her wings and she thinks it's uncool to go away with your parents, but she'll enjoy it when she gets there (after a bit of sulking!).

If she really digs her heels in, tell her she needs to find someone to stay with. I know some people would allow a sixteen-year-old to stay at home alone, but I wouldn't. I always think that if they were in bed at night and someone broke in or there was a fire, you'd realize just how young they are. If your daughter wants to stay at a friend's place and the parents are willing to take responsibility, then that would be the answer.

But make sure you speak to the parents direct. I used to say to Shane Junior that if he didn't want to come with us, I'd get an auntie to come and stay or I'd make him stay with a relative – that soon changed his mind!

Finally, if you decide to go away without her, don't give your daughter a key to the house. Shane was seventeen before we allowed him to have a key. It's not that we didn't trust him – we didn't trust other people. If you had a house to yourself for a week at that age, you'd throw a party, wouldn't you?

♥

## He's Jealous of His Friend's Foreign Holiday

**My eight-year-old son keeps asking why we can't go to Disney World on holiday this year where his school friend is going. We can't afford a trip like that and will be going to a British seaside resort instead. How can I help him to understand why we can't go and get him to look forward to our family holiday?**

Kids always want what their friends have – whether it's new trainers or a posh holiday. I think your son is old enough, though, to take on board why you can't go to Disney World. You don't have to burden him with your financial worries, but explain that you can't spend all your money on one holiday because you have lots of other things to pay for during the year – things that he enjoys, too, like after-school clubs, trips to the cinema, new clothes and so on. Explain that everyone has to work out how to spend their money wisely so they don't run out and can pay for all the things they like doing.

Next, get him excited about your staycation by putting a positive spin on it. Look up where you're going online or bring home some brochures and get him to write down all the things he wants to do on holiday and the places he'd like to visit. Then get him to write a little checklist of the things he'd like to pack or buy when he gets there such as a camera, a fishing net, a bucket and spade and so on. He'll soon get excited and be bragging to his friend about what he'll be doing this summer.

I bet he'll have a brilliant time. Some of my best family holidays have been spent by the British seaside. There's nothing quite like sitting on the seafront eating fish and chips wrapped in newspaper or having candy floss at the fair. If you're lucky the sun will shine, but, if not, being blown about by a force 10 gale as you watch the kids turn blue collecting crabs from rock pools has its own special charm!

Remember, not everyone in his class can afford to go to Florida, so he definitely won't be the only one holidaying at home.

SEVEN

# *Love and Loss*

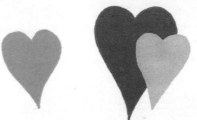

# Helping Your Kids Cope With Bereavement

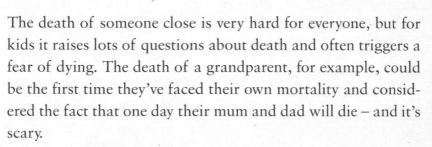

The death of someone close is very hard for everyone, but for kids it raises lots of questions about death and often triggers a fear of dying. The death of a grandparent, for example, could be the first time they've faced their own mortality and considered the fact that one day their mum and dad will die – and it's scary.

My philosophy has always been to be honest and open, and get them used to the idea of death early. It's natural to want to protect your children from the facts but, if you do this, it might come as a shock later on. Explain to them that dying is part of life and use examples like a dead bird or a dead goldfish to help them understand. I always think it's a good idea for children to have pets as they might experience the pet dying before they have to face the death of a relative.

When my son Jake developed a phobia of dying, I never lied to him or said, 'I'm never going to die.' But I reassured him by saying, 'Hopefully, I'll be very old when I do, so it won't be for many, many years.' That way it seemed a long way off and not something he should be worrying about now.

Losing someone close is hard on you, too, and you need time to grieve while supporting the kids. When my mum died, I explained to my children that there would be days when I'd cry so it didn't scare them and so I didn't have to bottle up my emotions.

Time is a great healer for kids as well as adults, but there are also lots of things you can do to prepare them for the loss of a loved one and to help them cope afterwards.

## Prepare Them Gradually

If a close friend or relative has a terminal illness, start talking to your child about it so they can get used to the idea gradually. If it's a grandparent who they spend lots of time with, make sure they start to spend time with other family members, too, so they're not left with a big hole in their lives when that person dies.

# Keep Talking to Them

After a loved one has died, tell them they can talk to you about anything they want and let them know it's OK to cry. They might not want to do it in front of you in case they upset you, but reassure them that you don't mind. Tell them you might cry, too, but that it's all right to be sad for a while.

If it's a parent they've lost, they may think it's because of something they did wrong, so reassure them it wasn't their fault. They might be frightened that you'll die, too, and become very clingy, so make it clear you don't expect anyone else – including yourself – to die. This is really tough on you as you'll be grieving for your partner as well as trying to help your kids, so make sure you have lots of supportive family and friends around you.

## Tell the School

Definitely inform their school if a close relative has died. Teachers are trained to help in these situations – they might read a special book about death with your child and they'll keep an eye on them to see how they're coping.

## Find Out How They Want to Say Goodbye

If they're old enough, ask how they feel about going to the funeral, but don't force them to go if they don't want to. Suggest they can take some flowers to the grave another time. Other nice ideas are lighting a candle in a church or next to a photo at home, planting a tree in memory of the person who's died, throwing a flower into the sea and letting the tide carry it away or releasing a balloon.

## Keep Memories Alive

Talk to them about all the memories they have of that person and the fun times they had together – I did this a lot with Ciara when her grandma died. I also put a photo of my mum up in the house so Ciara could see her whenever she wanted.

You could get them to make up a photo album so they have a focus for their emotions. Or they could fill a special memory box with items to help them remember the person – photos, souvenirs of places they visited together, birthday cards, a CD and so on. Writing a letter to the person who died is another good way of expressing how they feel. Ciara still writes to her grandma now.

It's also important to mark anniversaries like a birthday as well as the day the person died. Do anything that seems fitting – it could be taking the kids out of school for a special excursion or getting the whole family together for a meal to share happy memories.

## Keep Up Their Activities

It's important to give children a sense of stability through all the upheaval a death can cause, so try to keep their routine the same if possible. Make sure they get to do their normal activities like football or swimming lessons. It's even more important for teenagers to keep up their hobbies or find new interests – it'll give them a focus and help build up their confidence again.

## Watch Out for Signs They're Not Coping

Grief can show itself in lots of different ways. Younger children might act up, suffer from more tummy bugs than usual or want to talk about the person who's died all the time. Teenagers might skip school, become aggressive, drop their hobbies or have trouble sleeping. If you think any of this behaviour is going on too long, get some advice from your GP. It could be they need to talk to someone outside the family such as a counsellor. Cruse Bereavement Care has a young person's freephone helpline (0808 808 1677) and a website called Road For You (www.rd4u.org.uk) to support young people dealing with loss. It has message boards and even a special Lads Only section, which I think is a great idea because boys often find it so hard to open up and share what they're feeling.

Another good website is www.childbereavement.org.uk, which has lots of information for adults and young people that you can download. It also has a support line (01494 446648) and there are special DVDs and books which you can buy cheaply to help children and teenagers deal with different issues, including the death of a sibling, sudden death and terminal illness.

## Tell Them It's OK to Have Fun Again

Children might feel guilty about enjoying themselves after a bereavement, particularly if it's a brother or sister they've lost. Reassure them that you want them to get on with their lives and to be able to have fun and laugh again.

# My Son's Become a Hypochondriac Since His Granddad Died

**My twelve-year-old son is obsessed with the idea that he has something wrong with him. If he has a headache, he says: 'Do I have cancer?' I reassure him that he's fine, but I'm starting to worry he's turning into a hypochondriac. His grandfather died a few months ago and I think that may have affected him.**

I think the fact that his granddad passed away is absolutely why he's been acting like this. He's been confronted by death at the age of twelve and it's made him aware of his mortality. When I was around his age I was phobic about dying. I used to lie in bed worrying that if I went to sleep I'd never wake up. My mum used to tell me that the older I got, the less frightened I'd be and she was right. You could ask him if he'd feel better if he talked to a counsellor. That might seem a scary step, but I'm all for counselling and it might be just the thing to help your son if he's becoming more paranoid. Talk to your GP about a referral. It might not be a bad idea to take him to the doctor for a check-up anyway so he can be told he's fighting fit by an expert and not just by his mum. Something simple like that could be all he needs.

Don't dismiss what he's telling you, though. This is a real fear for him and it's very scary. Keep listening and giving him lots of reassurance.

# EIGHT

# *The Tween Years*

# Coping With Their Growing Independence

The tween years, from about nine to twelve, can be hard for you as a mum. All of a sudden your kids don't quite need you as much as they did. Their personalities are developing at a rate of knots and they're beginning to want more independence. There's the odd cheeky little comment creeping in, too – practising for when they hit the terrible teens! It's a really weird time because you still want them to be kids but they're turning into mini-adults before your very eyes. It's all about trying to find a balance between you wanting to hang on to their childhood for dear life and them wanting to grow up too quickly.

I'm seeing it with Ciara, who's eight-and-a-half. She's really into music now, getting her dad to download Lady Gaga and Katy Perry. It only seems like yesterday it was '*High School Musical* this, *High School Musical* that'; now it's all about sexy young women gyrating on stage in next to nothing, singing about kissing girls! I feel a bit sad because Ciara's my last child and I just don't want her to get older. It's as simple as that. She's started having sleepovers at her friend's house next door and she's so thrilled with herself because she feels grown-up. I'm happy for her, too, but now she's made the break, I realize there'll be no stopping her. At the moment, though, I'm consoling myself with the fact that she still believes in Santa. My sister's daughter stopped believing at about the age of nine, so I figure I still have one more year of leaving out the milk and carrots on Christmas Eve.

These years are also when your child develops a growing need for privacy. Ciara's started writing a little diary, which I'm not allowed to look in. She'll say, 'Mum, will you put this somewhere safe and don't let anyone read it?' Of course I'm desperate to read it! But I have no reason to. If I thought Ciara's behaviour had changed and she was dreading going to school, then I'd read it because I'd be worried about her, but she's dead happy.

Then there are the dreaded hormones! These start kicking in at about eleven or twelve. When my boys got to this age, that's when we started getting a bit of moodiness and backchat. I'm sure all mums of kids at this stage are familiar with that well-worn phrase, 'But it's not fair, my friends are allowed to do it!' Battles over room tidying with Shane and Jake ignited around then, too. They'd always say to me, 'It's my room, what's the problem?' To which I'd usually reply, 'It smells, that's the problem!' Often there'd be a half-eaten pizza under the bed, along with a whole load of dirty clothes they'd expect to magically reappear clean and folded in the drawer.

Expect your kids to start taking a much bigger interest in how they look, too. Every shopping trip for clothes will be a battle of wills from now on. And they start to develop little crushes on pop stars, teachers and each other!

Around the age of ten or eleven kids also start becoming more aware of their bodies and the inevitable questions about sex start cropping up, too. My philosophy has always been to be frank without going overboard on the detail. I would far rather they heard it from me than worry about it, or pick up the wrong information in the playground. I think I decided to be open and honest with my children because when I was growing up, subjects like puberty and sex were never discussed in our house. When I tried to ask my mum about the facts of life she wouldn't even talk to me about periods. So I let my kids know from an early age that I'd always be there to answer their questions.

When children get to this age it's really important to keep

lines of communication open and for them to feel comfortable talking to you about anything that's worrying them.

Luckily, when I got to eleven or twelve I had five older sisters to help me with the facts of life!

## How Can I Get Him to Tidy His Room?

**How can I get my twelve-year-old son to tidy his room? It's a disgusting tip, but it doesn't matter how much I nag, he never cleans it and, in the end, I always do it myself.**

Oh boy, do I know how you feel! I'm sorry to say it's not because he's twelve – they don't get much better with age.

I've spent years of my life nagging Shane and Jake and I usually give up in despair. But I have found that giving your child an incentive to tidy up can work. I've tried punishments, like not letting them go out with their friends, but then they hang around the house all day and punish me! So try a bit of extra pocket money. I know this sounds like bribery, but I think it's worth letting them earn money doing a chore. Be prepared for the fact that he might not do a very good job, but even if he puts his dirty laundry in the basket and takes dirty cups and plates to the kitchen, it's worth it.

In my experience, though, you'll have to finish off what he's started!

## My Three Ways To . . .
## Get Them to Do Chores

**Be tough.** The number-one thing is that you mustn't let them do anything else until they do their chores first. Emphasize that your family is a team and everyone has to pull together. Once they've done what you've asked, they can then go out to play or watch their favourite TV show. They'll soon realize the quicker they do it, the better.

**Make it fun.** Mundane chores such as putting the bins out can be dull, so try to make it fun. Stick on some music and challenge them to see who can put all their dirty washing in the laundry basket the fastest. Whatever the chore, if they feel like they're having fun, they won't mind doing it.

**Give them lots of praise.** Finally, no matter how well or badly the job is done, give them loads of praise. It'll boost their self-esteem and encourage a sense of responsibility. Plus, it'll make them more likely to do their chores without complaint next time.

## Should I Let Her Get Her Ears Pierced?

**My nine-year-old daughter wants to get her ears pierced and I'm not sure if I should let her. My mum wouldn't let me have mine done till I was sixteen, but perhaps that's over the top these days?**

Every time we go shopping Ciara will say, 'Mum, please can I have it done?' It's essentially because all the girls in her class have pierced ears. I'm not against it, but her dad is – he thinks it'll hurt too much. Personally I think earrings look nice on little girls and it's not like your daughter is saying she wants to wear a mini-skirt and a boob tube! It doesn't necessarily mean she's growing up too quickly and, if you're strict and only let her wear little studs and not long dangly earrings, I think it's fine.

However, at the end of the day, if you feel it's wrong, then stick to your guns and don't be pressured by a nine-year-old. My mum wouldn't let me get my ears pierced until I was twelve, so perhaps compromise and let her get them done at that age?

## Coping With Pester Power

Tweens are the prime years for kids pestering their parents for the latest fads and toys. I always tried to explain to my children that they didn't always have to have what their friends had to win a popularity contest. If you don't put your foot down over certain things they ask for, where is it going to stop?

A good way to find out if they really do want something, and it's not just their latest whim, is to suggest they save up their pocket money to buy it. You'll be surprised how quickly they don't want it! That happened so many times with my boys. Suddenly those ridiculous-looking trainers didn't seem quite so appealing after all!

# How Can I Get Him to Exercise?

**What can I do – short of bribery – to get my ten-year-old son to exercise? He's very lazy and prefers to slump in front of the TV or a computer game than do any activity.**

You've got to make exercise fun, so they don't even know they're doing it. If your son won't do it on his own, make it something you can do together, or get his friends involved.

Exercise can be just a brisk walk, a cycle ride, a game of badminton in the back garden or a trip to the park to play football or rounders. Begin slowly and try to build in some structured activity a couple of times a week or at weekends. Just walking to and from the school every day with him is a start. I think parents are much more conscious about exercise at the moment because child obesity is in the news such a lot. These days, most kids would prefer to watch telly or play a computer game, but remember they do have off buttons! I don't understand why parents forget who the boss is – just *tell* him he has to stop watching telly.

If you are going to bribe him, make sure it's in a positive way. Don't give him money or buy him things, otherwise he'll think he's got you under his thumb. Instead, say: 'If you go out today for an hour, you can watch TV or play on your computer for an extra ten minutes tonight when we get back.' Don't lapse and let him sit there for an hour – stay in control.

**SAFETY TIP!**

The internet can be a great place for your kids to learn, play and explore, but always make sure the computer is in a family room instead of their bedroom so you can monitor the sites they're using. Also invest in child-protection software that filters out any sites with sexual or violent content and can record chat-room messages, emails and even what's been typed. Your kids must know never to give out any personal information online, including their name, address, phone number, the name of their school or their internet passwords. Get them to use a child-friendly search engine like http://kids.yahoo.com.

## My Three Ways To . . . Reduce the Time Kids Spend On Their Computer

**Set limits.** Give them a time limit on the computer, which is down to your discretion. The first couple of times you enforce this there will be arguments, but they'll get used to it.

**Have a password.** If you make the computer password protected, they won't be able to sneakily use it behind your back and you'll know how long they're spending on it. Or simply unplug it, which is what I did with my boys.

**Inspire them elsewhere.** Try finding something else they're interested in and encourage it. It's important they realize there's more to life than computer games.

# How Do I Explain We're Short of Money?

**I lost my job a few months ago and although I did get another one, it's only part-time and not as well paid as before. My husband's hours have been cut too. We have two sons aged eight and ten and we're struggling to afford for them to carry on doing things like karate clubs, swimming lessons and going to football matches. How can I explain this to them?**

It must be a very worrying time for you, but I think your kids are old enough to understand a little about what's going on. Obviously, you don't have to tell them all the details and make them worried, but you can tell them that there are some things you can't afford any more.

Ask them to choose which activity they enjoy the most and want to stick with and say they'll have to put the others on hold for a while. Explain how you, too, have had to give up things you enjoy for the time being. You could also sit down as a family and write a list of the things you all need and want. Sort out all the 'needs' first for everyone, then move on to the extras. This will help the kids feel involved and that they're doing something to help.

Kids are far more adaptable than adults and I'm sure if you tackle the problem in these ways, they'll understand and be less daunted by any changes to their routine.

## My Three Ways To . . .
## Teach Them the Value of Money

**Give them an allowance.** Work out how much you spend on them each week buying treats, clothes and so on. Give them that amount in cash and tell them it's up to them to manage it. If they run out, don't give them any more.

**Pay them for doing extra chores.** Paying them to do things like washing your car or tidying up the garden will teach them a good lesson about working and earning. It's important for them to understand that nothing comes for free.

**Encourage them to save.** Get them to put money aside in a piggy bank for a special reason such as spending money for a holiday or a game they've had their eye on. Or take them to the bank to open their first savings account and get them to keep track of how well they're doing with a savings book or by checking their balance online.

# Let's Talk About the Birds and the Bees

When it comes to discussing sex with your tween, my advice is to let them take the lead and answer their questions when they arise. Think of it as being an ongoing process rather than one big scary sit-down talk. Here are some tips for nervous parents.

- **Create the right environment.** Try to create an atmosphere at home where your child can ask about sex, for example, when a story about sex crops up on a TV soap. Use informal opportunities like these to address issues surrounding the subject.
- **Talk about love.** Discuss sex in the context of loving relationships and use events like the birth of a baby or a wedding to talk about responsibility to others.
- **Be honest.** Don't just say, 'People have sex to make babies.' Explain that people also do it because they enjoy it and it feels good.
- **Be alert to puberty.** Although most girls get their first period between the ages of thirteen and fourteen, some can get it as young as eight. As the mum of an eight-year-old girl this seems ridiculously young, but they need to know what

to expect so they're not alarmed. The same goes for boys, who need to know about erections and wet dreams.

- **Don't be embarrassed.** If it's obvious you're squirming with embarrassment talking to them about sex, they'll feel awkward about bringing it up with you.
- **Teach respect.** Tell them sex is something that both people must want and that everyone has the right to say 'no'.
- **Talk about unwanted touching.** Explain to them that no one has the right to touch them and that they must tell you straightaway if it happens.
- **Get help!** If you do find it difficult to talk about sex with your child, use an age-appropriate book or website, which you can go through together. Visit www.thehormonefactory.com, which is a really fun site aimed at ten- to twelve- year-olds where they can take quizzes and get answers in a lighthearted way.

# She Heard Us Having Sex

**I overheard my nine-year-old telling her friend she'd heard me and her father having sex. I didn't even know she knew what sex was! I'm really embarrassed and wonder whether I should bring it up with her in case she's confused or worried. Have you any ideas?**

It can be traumatic to hear your mum and dad having sex when you're nine, but to make a big deal of it wouldn't improve things. Perhaps she was telling her friend in an 'Oh my God!' way and thought it was funny. But if you notice a change in her mood, then it's time to talk. If she's clingy or withdrawn it could be because she didn't like what she heard. In that case, bring it up gently. Perhaps ask, 'Have you got something on your mind? Why are you so quiet?' Hopefully she'll just say, 'I heard you and Daddy making noises.' Then you can explain it.

I understand it's embarrassing – and it can be hard to explain things without sounding crude, but you don't have to go into detail. If you feel you don't know how to answer her questions, there are great books aimed specifically at helping you to talk to your children about sex in a way that's right for their age, and you can use them as an aid to discuss it. A good book that other mums have recommended to me is *Let's Talk About Sex* by Robie H. Harris, which is aimed at kids from nine years old.

Once you've addressed it, move on. She probably won't dwell on it for very long – nine-year-olds have plenty more important things on their minds like *Hannah Montana*, computer games, new clothes and so on.

## She Wants a Sleepover With Her Male Friend

**I'm a single dad bringing up my twelve-year-old daughter. She has asked me if a boy who is a friend can stay overnight in her room if we put a bed down for him. This boy is fourteen and very nice, but I've said no. She asked me why, as her girl pals have always stayed in her room for sleepovers. What can I say to her without having a big discussion on underage sex? And if I do have this talk and she says I don't trust her, how do I explain my decision then?**

When Jake was fifteen, he had a thirteen-year-old girlfriend and she stayed at our house, but I would never let them sleep in the same room. It's different when they're little, but at twelve and fourteen they're going through puberty and they know more than they let on, I can tell you. Even if your daughter is saying they're only friends, can you be sure she means it?

At the moment she's far too young to have boys staying

over, end of story. You don't need to explain it because you're her father and you're the boss. If you're OK with him staying, then fine – he can sleep in the spare room.

Sometimes being a parent is rubbish because you end up being the big bad wolf – but that's just how it is. You don't say if your daughter has had her first period yet, but if she has there's the risk of an unwanted pregnancy if they do have sex. Think about how you'd feel if that happened.

It must be tough as a single dad bringing up a daughter who's going through puberty, but maybe you can enlist a female family friend or relative to talk to her about sex and answer any questions she has, as she might feel too shy to ask you.

## He Gets So Homesick

**My son is nearly nine and going on his first school camping trip next week. He gets really homesick and I'm worried he won't enjoy the experience. He's too embarrassed to talk to his friends or his teachers about it. What can I say to reassure him?**

Tell him there are probably another five of his friends who all feel the same way, who are also too embarrassed to discuss it.

I think it's harder for boys. Girls will talk to each other about their emotions but boys bottle it up.

I remember when Jake went on his first school trip at that age. I just kept telling him what a fantastic time he would have and reminding him I was just at the end of the phone if he needed me. I also made a special effort to build up his confidence by telling him the trip would only last a few days and he'd come back having had a great time with all his friends. Have a quiet word with your son's teacher. Say: 'Don't tell him I told you this, but please can you look out for him, he doesn't want his friends to know.'

When Jake went on his trip, I let him pick out a book to take with him. I told him: 'If you can't sleep, then read the book and let your imagination focus on that rather than being homesick.' Another good idea is to get your son to write a letter that he never has to show anyone explaining all his feelings. You could give him a family photo to take, although that could make him miss you more.

Get excited about the trip yourself and tell him what a great adventure it will be, and that he'll soon be back to tell you all about it.

# He Hates Wearing His Glasses

**My ten-year-old son is short-sighted and needs glasses, but he's really self-conscious and hates wearing them. How can I make him feel better about himself?**

My daughter Ciara really wanted glasses the last time I took her to the opticians. It seems having braces and glasses is the in-thing among her friends at the moment! There are so many really trendy frames now for kids, so try to get your son excited about choosing a pair and buy him the ones he's picked himself – even if you think they're awful! Kids start to worry about what they look like at this age, so it's important he feels in control of choosing the frames and is comfortable wearing them.

Then do everything else you can to boost his confidence – point out all the really cool celebrities who wear glasses and give him extra support with his schoolwork and hobbies.

# I'm Worried About Him Starting High School

**I'm concerned that my sensitive eleven-year-old son will struggle when he moves to a large comprehensive. He was teased a bit at primary school and is worried about it happening again. Do you have any advice?**

I was also concerned when my son Jake began secondary school. He had sleepless nights because he was told a boy there wanted to batter him. The best thing to do is speak to the headmaster to make sure your son will be properly supported and find out who he can talk to if there's a problem. I explained to Jake's headmaster that he was a bit nervous and told him about this other kid. The head was brilliant and said he would keep an eye on the situation and I should tell Jake his teachers would be looking out for him.

I also reassured Jake that if, at any stage, he was being bullied and the teachers couldn't deal with it, I would take him out of the school. I made sure he knew I wouldn't let anything happen to him.

In the end the strangest thing happened. Within two weeks of starting, Jake and this boy became best friends and the boy often stayed at our house.

It's tough, though, when your child starts secondary school.

The first few weeks will be tricky as your son finds his way and starts to make friends. The main thing for you to do is not to show you're worried or he'll pick up on it and worry even more himself. If you're anything like me, you'll be stressed out that first day. But the chances are he'll come bounding back and tell you lots of stories about all the things he did. It might take him time to settle in, but moving schools could be just what he needs to build his confidence. After all, it's a chance for him to make a fresh start away from those bullies at primary school and meet a whole new group of friends.

For more on this, see Beating the Bullies on page 215.

## My Three Ways to Ease the Move to High School

**Take away the fear.** Your child's primary school should arrange a visit to the secondary school so things don't seem quite so scary for them on that first day. If not, maybe you should team up with a few other mums and arrange a visit yourself so the kids become familiar with the building and the route to school.

**Find them an older buddy.** If your child doesn't have an older sibling attending the school, get together with friends who have kids at the school so your child can ask them questions about what to expect. It might make them feel better to know they have an older friend already at the school.

**Give extra support while they settle in.** Keep an eye on how they're getting on during those first few weeks – ask lots of questions about new activities, subjects and friends. They will also be getting more homework than they're used to, so make sure you're there to encourage and help them.

# How Can I Get Him to Do His Homework?

**My eleven-year-old son will not get down to his homework after school. He'll do anything else. It's becoming a real cause of friction at home and I'm worried his grades will start to suffer. Have you any advice?**

Shane Junior says now that the only reason he got all his GCSEs was because Ray was always so strict with him when it came to doing homework. Ray would say, 'You're not going out till you've done your homework, then the rest of the night is yours.' He'd let Shane and Jake have a half-hour chill-out when they got home in the afternoon, then they'd have to get down to it. And they'd do it because they realized it made sense. When I was a kid, I'd sit around all night, dreading doing my homework and of course the whole night would be wasted.

If you stick to your guns over this, your son will get into a routine and he'll want to finish his homework so he can do something he enjoys. A good homework and learning site for kids to try is www.bbc.co.uk/schools. Here are a few more tips to make things a little easier:

- **Give them a break.** They'll need a little time after school to relax and have a drink and a snack to keep them going until tea.

- **Find a good study space.** They'll need quiet to concentrate, so set up somewhere for homework that's away from the TV and other distractions. It'll get done quicker, too!
- **Ask them if they need any help.** It's no good telling them to do it if you're not around to give them pointers.
- **Praise them when they've done it.** Check their homework, then tell them to put their books away and enjoy themselves for the rest of the evening.

♥

## Should I Let Her Travel at Twelve?

**My twelve-year-old daughter is going to a summer disco with friends. She wants to go there in a taxi but I want to give them a lift there and back. Am I right to worry?**

I think it's fine to let her go by taxi. It'll be daylight and if they all meet first at someone's house, then they can set off in the taxi together. It's her way of feeling like a grown-up and I wouldn't have a problem with that.

But as for coming back, that's another matter. I'd insist on picking her up. I used to let my boys travel to events by taxi, then I'd meet them at the end of the evening. As far as I'm concerned, it's non-negotiable. If it's an under-sixteens disco she's going to, they normally finish at 10 p.m., so get there a bit earlier so you're there when she comes out. I remember when I used to pick up the boys, I'd see kids hanging around waiting for cabs or walking home and it really worried me. They may think they're grown-up, and some of them may even look a lot older than they are, but if anything bad happened would they know what to do?

If your daughter is embarrassed about her mum picking her up, then why not do a deal? Arrange to meet her just round the corner so her friends won't see her getting in the car with you.

## Keeping Your Tween Safe

Now your child is becoming increasingly independent, it's important they know some basic safety rules for when they're out and about on their own. They should:

- **Know their numbers.** Your tween should know their address, home phone number and how to dial 999 in an emergency.
- **Get mobile.** If you have an older tween who has a mobile phone, put your home number on speed dial and make sure their battery is charged up when they leave the house. It's also a good idea to add contact details of one or two other trusted adults who they can call in an emergency.

- **Be street savvy.** Make sure they know how to be safe when crossing roads. Emphasize they must be alert at all times and never cross the road while listening to an MP3 player or talking on their mobile phone.
- **Keep you informed.** Make sure they always tell you where they're going and with whom. Keep a list of their friends' parents' phone numbers handy, too.
- **Be alert to strangers.** There's no need to frighten the life out of them, but make sure they know to shout as loudly as they can and run away if a stranger tries to take them somewhere.
- **Know what to do if they're lost.** Tell them to find a police officer, a shop assistant or a grown-up with kids to ask for help.

♥

## Should I Let Him Stay Up Late?

**My son has just turned twelve and is begging me to move his bedtime from 9 p.m. to 10.30. I think this is too late, but am I being unreasonable?**

You should compromise. Why don't you agree that his bedtime is 9.30 p.m. on week nights, but at the weekend he can stay up till 10.30? If I had it my way, kids of your son's age would be tucked up by 9 p.m., but I am unrealistic. Things are not like they were when I was twelve. Jake's bedtime used to be 9.30 but when he turned thirteen we agreed to push it back half an hour.

If your son reacts badly when you suggest 9.30, then just be firm. At the end of the day it's for his own good.

## Sibling Rivalry . . . It's Gone Into Overdrive!

The tween years were when sibling rivalry really went up a gear in our house. At one point I couldn't leave Shane and Jake alone because I was worried they'd put each other in hospital!

I remember one day walking into the house to find Shane trying to hold the lounge door closed while Jake was standing on the other side of it holding one of Shane's football trophies; he wanted to batter him with it. Shane knew all the right buttons to press with his younger brother and sometimes I'd have to pull them apart. As their mum it was heartbreaking and I thought they were never going to get on with each other. Now

I'm very happy – and relieved – to report they're the best of friends and are always Facebooking and texting each other.

Of course all mums want their kids to like each other, but sometimes siblings are very different and you have to accept they might grow up to love each other and have a healthy respect for each other, but they'll never be close.

How you deal with sibling rivalry when they're kids, though, can make a huge difference to how they get along as teenagers and even as adults, so it's very important to stay calm and remain fair at all times. Here are a few pointers.

- **Remember it's normal.** They're trying to find out where they feature in the pecking order – who's the leader of the pack? It's just them jockeying for position inside the family.
- **Always be fair.** Try to give them an equal amount of time and praise. If one of your kids excels at sport then make sure you find something the other is good at. Shane was good at football but then we found that Jake was good at drama – and both received equal praise for everything they did.
- **Tell them it's not a competition.** Remind them you love them both equally and there's no need to compete. And, if one is getting praise or attention, don't forget to include the other, too.
- **Get them to sort it out.** If they've had a dispute, encourage them to sort it out themselves so they learn to find ways of

reaching a compromise. Tell them you'll act as referee if they need you.

- **Step in if it gets nasty.** Make it clear that any kind of physical violence is unacceptable – that means no kicking, biting or hitting. If this happened with my boys, I'd take away one of their privileges or send them to their rooms to cool off.
- **Never compare them.** Don't talk about one child in front of the other or compare them in front of other people.
- **All join in.** Do as much as you can together as a family to help your kids bond – it could be anything from board games to bike rides.
- **Banish boredom.** Squabbling tends to reach new heights during times when they're bored, such as school holidays, so do what you can to keep them busy.

# NINE

# *Beating the Bullies*

# Fighting Back Without Fists

Even now I can still remember what it felt like being at the mercy of the playground bully. It was horrible. He used to deliberately trip me up or push and shove me, so I'd always have grazes on my knees. One day something inside me just snapped and I screamed at him to leave me alone. In the end he did and that is often the case. Bullies are actually quite cowardly, so when you confront them they back off.

I wouldn't recommend confronting a bully today, though, after reading so many terrible stories about children being happy-slapped or attacked with knives. As a mum it just doesn't bear thinking about. There are ways to respond, though, that don't involve getting into an argument with a bully or hitting back. When my sisters became famous with the Nolans, I started getting comments at school like, 'Your sisters can't sing!' and I learnt very quickly to respond with something like, 'Yeah, you're right, I don't like them either.'

My sons had similar problems with bullies at school because of who their parents are. They were always getting told me and their dad Shane were 'rubbish on the telly'. So I taught them to deflect the nasty comments by firing back quick one-liners. They'd say, 'Yeah, whatever . . .' or 'Yeah, they are rubbish, aren't they?' I told them never to worry about saying those things because I knew they loved me. It worked. By pretending to be indifferent or replying with a funny response there was no weak side for the bullies to target, so they eventually got bored trying.

Of course, kids don't always tell anyone they're being bullied because they're frightened of getting into more trouble or they feel ashamed, so it's important to recognize signs of trouble. One day Ciara said she had stomachache and felt sick in the morning, so I kept her off school, but a little later in the day she was absolutely fine. When I questioned her about it, she admitted she was being picked on, so I spoke to the head-teacher. Thankfully, it stopped straight away, but I'm now extra vigilant. Other tell-tale signs your child could be being bullied include 'lost' dinner money or possessions, cuts and bruises, not wanting to go to school and being withdrawn or bad-tempered.

Try to get them to confide in you by asking gentle questions about their day at school, such as what they did at lunchtime or playtime, who their friends are and if there's anyone in their class they don't like and why. I know from experience how upsetting and worrying it is to find out your child is being bullied, but there are ways to tackle the problem.

- **Take it seriously.** If your child tells you they're being bullied, it's probably taken a lot of courage, so take what they say seriously. Talk to the school as soon as you can – they might have no idea what is happening, but most schools these days are good at dealing with bullying. Teenagers may be embarrassed about you going to their school and ask you to forget it. That happened with my son Jake, so I saw his teachers on the quiet and asked them to keep an eye on him. It made all the difference.
- **Keep talking.** If your child is being bullied, keep calm in your dealings with both them and the school. It's natural to be angry and want to leap to the defence of the one you love, but it is also important to listen to both sides so you can find a solution quickly.
- **Get support from friends.** Encourage your child's friendships – invite their mates over for tea or sleepovers regularly. Joining an after-school club such as karate, swimming or football might help them find new friends and build their confidence, too.
- **Advise them to stick with their mates.** Tell them to staywith their friends during break times at school. Bullies are cowardly and generally won't pick on another kid if there are lots of other people around to witness it.
- **Tell them it's OK to speak up.** Make sure they know not to

fight back – that'll only encourage the bully and they could get hurt. Instead, advise them to identify a teacher they like at school who they can speak to if they're being threatened.

- **Be there for them.** Do everything you can to boost your child's self-esteem – encourage them in what they're good at and praise them when they do things well. Let them know how much you love them and that you're always there to listen. When Jake was being picked on at school, I made sure he knew I'd never let anything bad happen and that we'd find a new school if that's what it took.

## The Curse of Cyber Bullying

These days kids can be abused or intimidated via text, email, chatrooms or social networking sites. This may mean anything from threatening messages to posting humiliating photos online so others can join in the bullying. I've always felt really strongly that children shouldn't be given mobile phones or computers too early and this is another good reason for not giving in when they pester you for them.

If your child or teen is a victim of cyber bullying, tell them not to respond (bullies just love a reaction) but to keep the messages. Networking sites and internet providers can trace bullies and ban them. You should also change your child's mobile phone number and email address and only give it out to people you trust.

Kids can check out www.cybermentors.org.uk, a site where young people support each other online.

## What To Do When Your Child's the Bully

Parents often can't believe their children are bullies – let's face it, none of us wants to think of our little angel being cruel or violent. But if you've been told that your child is bullying, you have to confront it and find ways to help them so they stop. Here are my tips on tackling it:

- Talk to their teacher to find out exactly what's been happening and try to work out if there are any reasons or triggers for their aggressive behaviour. Could they be feeling vulnerable or upset themselves and that's why they're taking things out on other kids? Make it clear to them the bullying has to stop immediately and keep in touch with the school to make sure that happens.
- At home, have very strict rules that mean nasty behaviour towards other people is totally unacceptable. Make sure they understand you won't tolerate it and there will be consequences if they are mean – try grounding them or stopping their pocket money or allowance.

- Help them to understand they must respect others and treat people as they'd like to be treated themselves.
- Ask yourself if your child could have picked up the bullying behaviour from someone in the family. If that's the case, you need to address it straightaway.
- Make them apologize to the children they've been bullying in person so they're facing up to what they've done.
- It's also important to be really positive about any good behaviour and help them find activities and hobbies they can focus their energy on. Hopefully, they'll find something they love doing and it'll give their self-esteem such a boost, they won't want to bully any more.

## More Info

Visit www.beatbullying.org, which has good advice for young people and parents. Kids can call Childline free on 0800 11 11 to speak to someone in confidence about bullying.

## My Son's Out Of Control

**My twelve-year-old son has been terrorizing a few of the other kids in his class. It started off with threats, but recently I've been called to the school because he's hit a couple of children. When I confront him he just becomes defensive and starts blaming the other kids for 'starting it'. What can I do?**

You have to nip this in the bud right away. He sounds like a very angry boy and there must be something at the root of his violent behaviour. He doesn't seem keen to open up to you, so I think you need to speak to his teacher again and get a school counsellor or social worker involved. Hopefully they'll be able to work out what's causing his aggression and help him.

Even though you're angry with him and he needs to realize you won't allow him to continue to terrorize other kids, it's also important to let him know you still love him and you'll support him while you tackle his bullying.

TEN

# *Surviving Divorce and Stepfamilies*

# Tears, Traumas and Happy Endings!

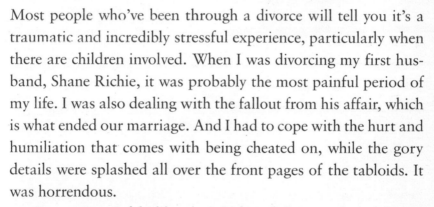

Most people who've been through a divorce will tell you it's a traumatic and incredibly stressful experience, particularly when there are children involved. When I was divorcing my first husband, Shane Richie, it was probably the most painful period of my life. I was also dealing with the fallout from his affair, which is what ended our marriage. And I had to cope with the hurt and humiliation that comes with being cheated on, while the gory details were splashed all over the front pages of the tabloids. It was horrendous.

As a mum I felt like a complete failure and was horrified my boys were going to be from a broken home. On top of everything I was going through with my ex, I couldn't shake this terrible guilt that I'd let my children down. My motherly instincts kicked in and all I wanted to do was protect Shane Junior, who was seven at the time, and Jake, who was only four.

Divorce is never going to be easy on the kids, but you can make it a lot less painful. The thing I was determined never to do was to get revenge on Shane through the boys. That would have been the easiest thing to do – to turn round and say, 'You're not seeing your kids.' You may think you're hurting your ex by doing that but, actually, you're just hurting the children. I'm not saying it's easy, especially when you tell the kids off for being naughty and they scream, 'I want Dad!' It's really hard not to turn round and say something like, 'Well, you can't have him, because he's with his girlfriend.'

So Shane could see the boys whenever he wanted and for as long as he wanted. There were no restrictions. Of course sometimes when he came over to pick them up, I wanted to open the door and punch him in the face! But it's really important to keep your feelings about your ex away from your children. Save it for a night out with the girls when you can have a few glasses of wine and really let rip!

I never bad-mouthed Shane in front of the boys and I never cried on their little shoulders. I kept their lives exactly the same – they never missed a Sunday football match or any school activity. It's so important to maintain their routine so their lives remain as unchanged as possible. If the kids see you crying into a wine glass every night and they're missing all their usual activities or not getting up for school on time, then that's really going to damage them.

# When It's Time to Move On

Even if you do everything you can to protect your children, divorce is still going to be disruptive and upsetting for them, but I believe it's still preferable to subjecting them to the fallout from an unhappy marriage. I kept my marriage going longer than I should have 'because of the kids'. You hear people say that all the time, but it's the wrong thing to do. It was going to counselling that helped me realize that.

My counsellor asked me if I really wanted to bring my kids up to think the sort of marriage we had was all right. Or whether I wanted my boys to grow up, meet a girl, mess her about and then say to me, 'Well, what are you moaning about?' because they'd seen their dad treat me that way. And of course the answer was no. It's a terrible example to set.

While you're in the middle of a divorce it's hard to imagine anything good happening again, but I'm living proof that it can change your life in a positive way. If my first marriage hadn't ended, I wouldn't have met and married Ray or had our lovely daughter, Ciara. I probably wouldn't have had the confidence to rebuild my career and achieve all the things I have done since. I'm not saying I didn't shed a lot of tears in the process, but it's important to realize there's always light at the end of the tunnel. And, when you're going through the worst times, there are also things you can do to make the journey a little easier.

## My Ten Ways to Make a Break-Up Less Painful for Them and for You

1. **Stay civil.** Even if you're seething with rage inside, try to behave in a civilized way towards your ex from the start to avoid the kids being traumatized by arguments. And never try to make them take sides. They love their dad and have the right to a good relationship with him.
2. **Be honest.** Try to be as truthful as you can with your kids about the break-up from the beginning – without going into the details – and reassure them they are loved by both of you and will still see both of you.
3. **Tell them it's not their fault.** All kids assume it must be something to do with them if their parents split up, so they need lots of reassurance.
4. **Keep their lives the same.** Divorce is hard on children emotionally so try to keep everything else in their lives un-

changed – keep them at the same school if possible and carry on with all their usual routines and activities, which will help them feel secure. I made sure I did this with my boys.

5. **Lean on friends.** Have a good support network of caring friends you can confide in so you don't end up using your children as a crutch. It's wrong and damaging, even if your kids are older, to burden them with your problems. And make sure you maintain their relationships with grandparents, aunts and uncles, so they have adult relatives other than you if they need someone to talk to.
6. **Agree on discipline.** Children like consistency and routine, so agree with your ex on issues such as which TV programmes are suitable, when they're allowed treats and what time they should go to bed. This will help avoid the kids playing you off against each other, too! There's nothing more annoying than hearing, 'But Dad said it was OK!'
7. **Be good to yourself.** There's nothing like a break-up to send your self-esteem into a nosedive – my divorce totally shattered my confidence. So, even if all you feel like doing is sitting around in your dressing gown eating chocolate biscuits, make the effort to do something nice for yourself. Get a new haircut, buy a pair of killer heels and say 'Yes' when your friends ask you to go out. It sounds daft, but all these things will help you find yourself again and boost your confidence.

8. **Consider counselling.** This really helped me when I was going through my divorce. It was great to be able to talk to someone who was completely unrelated to the situation and who was there just to listen to me. It helped me solve problems and cope with destructive emotions. Anger and bitterness are exhausting and the only person they hurt is you. Your GP can refer you to a counsellor, or visit the British Association for Counselling and Psychotherapy at www.bacp.co.uk to find a qualified therapist in your area.
9. **Contact a third party.** If you can't agree with your ex when it comes to access or money, a mediation service can help you reach joint decisions. Contact National Family Mediation at www.nfm.org.uk, which has offices nationwide.
10. **Agree to be friends.** Every break-up is different and staying friends with your ex isn't always possible, but, if you can, it's the best thing for you and your kids. I'm on friendly terms with Shane now and it makes things much easier for all of us because he's so involved with the boys' lives. He sent a message of congratulations when I got married to Ray and wished me good luck when I competed in *Dancing on Ice*.

# Learning to Live in a Stepfamily: When Ray Met the Boys

The only thing more traumatic than my divorce was settling into a new life with Ray and the boys. I remember when I first introduced them. 'This is my friend, Ray,' I said to Shane and Jake. 'He's not your friend, he's your boyfriend,' Shane replied moodily.

Jake would regularly come out with things like, 'Well, I never want my mum to meet anyone,' and Ray would be sitting there thinking, 'Oh my God, these kids hate me!'

The boys were just trying to protect me and letting Ray know he was on their territory – after all, they'd had me all to themselves for two years since I'd split up with their dad.

It took a good two years of really hard work from all of us for things to calm down. Some days were fantastic and others were absolute hell! But I think that's what you have to expect at first. Your kids will take time to get used to your new partner and he'll take time to get used to them. Everyone's trying to work out what the rules are. You're all getting to know each other and learning to live in the same house.

It was hard on Ray, especially because Shane was still very much in the picture – he had to be for the boys.

I felt stuck in the middle – a lot! I remember coming home some days when Ray had been looking after Shane Junior and Jake, and there'd been a row. None of them would talk to me because they wanted me to side with them. Funny how I ended up being blamed for everything!

One rule I made from very early on was never to disagree with Ray about discipline in front of the boys. I felt it was important for me to back his authority. At the same time, if I didn't agree with the way Ray had handled a situation, I'd wait until the boys were out of the room, then I'd say to him, 'I think you've been too harsh.'

Now, of course, Ray and the boys adore each other. And I've never felt he loves Ciara more than the boys – he's just as strict and loving with each of them.

Those first few years are make or break, though, and it doesn't surprise me that a quarter of stepfamilies split up in the first year. How we stayed together I'll never know! Every stepfamily is different and you have to find your own ways of settling into relationships with each other. You must be patient and understand that both kids and step-parents will take time to adjust – and inevitably there will be tears, traumas and tantrums along the way!

However, there are a few golden rules when you embark on that new relationship which should stand you in good stead for the future.

- **RULE 1. Take it slow.** Don't rush to introduce your new man to your kids, especially if they're still getting used to living apart from their dad. They need time to become accustomed to the idea that you could love someone else.
- **RULE 2. Ask: 'Will it last?'** Make sure your new relationship is a keeper before letting your children become attached to your new partner.
- **RULE 3. Reassure them he's not a replacement.** Make it clear your new man will never, ever replace their dad. My boys grew to love and respect Ray, but I never forced them to accept him as Dad Number Two.
- **RULE 4. Have alone time with your kids.** Make sure you spend plenty of quality time with your children away from your new partner to help them feel loved and secure.
- **RULE 5. Accept there will be bad behaviour.** A new man on the scene can be a huge shock to your children, especially if they're still getting used to all the upheaval your divorce caused. Naturally, they might feel insecure and worried about anyone taking you away from them. So don't be surprised if they have angry outbursts, become clingy or suddenly go down with mysterious tummy bugs when it's time to go to school. Talk to them sympathetically about how they're feeling and reassure them.
- **RULE 6. Take it easy when it comes to a permanent move.** Don't be too hasty to move your partner in and discuss it

with your kids first. Give them the opportunity to talk about any worries, particularly if your partner has children who'll be moving in or coming to stay regularly.

## He's So Rude to My New Partner

**I'm a single mum with two sons, aged thirteen and sixteen. I got divorced nine years ago and have only recently started a serious relationship. The man I'm seeing is wonderful, but my thirteen-year-old is rude to him. How can I help my son understand that he has nothing to be jealous of?**

If the relationship is serious, the best thing you can do is to sit down with your son and talk to him. Explain that your love for him will never change, even though you have a new man in your life. I remember saying to Shane: 'You want me to be happy, don't you? In a few years you'll be off doing your own thing and I will be on my own.' Reassure your son that you still love him and that nothing about your relationship has changed. If your partner moves in, then it can be difficult for a child to accept they have to listen to your new partner's rules, too.

It may be a good idea for you all to sit down and let your son talk about his fears so that he knows that you and your partner are taking his feelings into account – but not to the point where your son rules the roost.

It's hard, but it gets better with time, I promise.

## My Boyfriend Hates My Children

**My boyfriend doesn't seem to like my children – aged six and eight. I don't know what to do. Have you got any ideas?**

He hates your kids? Dump him. End of story. Your kids come first. When your boyfriend took you on, he took them on as well.

Having said that, if your kids are trying to make his life difficult – and he's stung by it – that's slightly different. Children can react badly when a new partner's on the scene. They're used to having you all to themselves and a stranger makes them jealous.

The main thing is whether your boyfriend is willing to try to make it work. If he is, then you might be able to work it out. Get everyone to sit down and discuss what you can do.

Always include the kids so they don't feel left out. When I got together with Ray, Jake was six. There were times when Jake was lovely to him and other times when he wasn't. I kept having to reassure him, 'I can't make you like Ray, I can only hope you will and whatever you decide I will always love you. You will always be my son. He's not coming in to take your place but to be part of the family.' Reassure your children they will always be number one and that he's not trying to be their dad, he's their mate. And of course, Jake and Ray are close now.

If it's just the case that your boyfriend doesn't like them, though, then end it. You can't let him come between you and the children – no man is worth that.

## They Act Up When They've Seen Their Dad

**I'm a single mum with two boys aged ten and twelve. I separated from their dad five years ago and they stay with him every other weekend. I have brought them up to be well-mannered but their dad is a lot more 'relaxed'. When they come back from his house they're unruly and rude and it's a few days before their behaviour returns to normal. What can I do?**

Every mum and dad will differ slightly in the way they believe their kids should be brought up, and kids are incredibly clever at picking up any inconsistencies and using those for their own benefit. But although they might think they're having a great time and getting away with murder, in the long run it can be unsettling to have two very different sets of ground rules. Try asking your ex if he'll agree to get together on neutral ground and come up with some guidelines that you can both live with – but remember, you have to compromise, too.

It'll be worth it if your kids aren't constantly having to swing from one extreme to the other.

## What If You're the Stepmum?

I know how hard it can be for step-parents after seeing what Ray had to contend with when he came to live with us. Simply by being there you've destroyed all hope the kids had of their parents getting back together again. So take things slowly – patience and understanding will help you win them over.

I've spoken to lots of stepmums and they all say the temptation at first is to over-indulge the kids with treats and presents because you want them to like you and don't want to be seen as the wicked stepmother! But if you're going to be a figure of authority in their lives you need them to respect you, too, and you don't want them to associate you just with treats. You also have to accept that the family you're moving into will already have established routines. However, if you're bringing your own kids into the home, it's a good idea to sit down to draw up some house rules, covering everything from bedtimes and discipline to curfews. It'll help everyone feel involved, too.

Don't expect to love your stepchildren the way you love your own kids. This might come with time, but it's best to be realistic and aim for a fulfilling, healthy relationship with them. Of course there will be tears and conflicts, but don't take it personally. They're just reacting against all the changes, not against you, and probably just want reassurance that they're still loved by their parents. Take it from me, if you can create a happy household most of the time, you're doing a brilliant job!

Finally, remember you're not alone – you have your partner to help take the strain. It's important to be able to confide in each other and work together to solve conflicts, but it's also vital to have regular nights out where you don't discuss your stepfamily situation at all. It was a lifeline for me and Ray.

## And Then There Was One: Sometimes It's No Fun As a Single Mum!

I'd been on my own for two years when I met Ray, so I'd had plenty of time to get used to being a single mum. Looking after the boys was exhausting sometimes, but in all honesty I found that part easy – at least they kept me busy and I was determined not to let them down by falling to pieces. Of course there were days when I felt really sorry for myself and I couldn't have got through those times without my mates. On days when I felt really down they'd be straight round. Friends and family are invaluable when you're left holding the baby – to help with practicalities like childcare and just to be there as a shoulder to cry on.

One thing my friends helped me to realize was that I was still a young woman with my whole life ahead of me – not just a mum who was there to clean the house, do the laundry and cook dinner.

The first year after my divorce I didn't think much about the future or meeting new men – I just tried to cope with each day, but slowly I felt more like rejoining society! Without my friends, though, I possibly wouldn't have got out of that rut. They'd come round and say, 'Right, get your glad rags on, we've got a babysitter and we're going out.' The thought of getting all dolled up was horrific when all I wanted to do was curl up in front of the telly, but I'm glad now I made the effort. I must admit, though, sometimes I'd come home feeling even more depressed because I'd been in a club with 400 blokes and hadn't fancied one of them! Just before I met Ray I'd decided to give up on pubs and clubs and thought, 'If I meet someone, great, but if I don't, then me and the boys will be fine on our own.' It was amazing how much more relaxed I became when I wasn't 'trying' to meet anyone . . . then I bumped into Ray in a bar and we got talking because he knew my niece. The rest, as they say, is history!

ELEVEN

# Teenage Kids

# The Trials and Tribulations of Growing Up

If you thought the Terrible Twos was a tricky age, just try being the mum of a teen. It's no myth: they really do go through that 'Kevin the Teenager' stage where they stop talking to you and just grunt when you ask them a question. When you say anything at all to them, their eyes go up to heaven, as if to say, 'What do you know?' They sleep late at weekends – in fact, any day of the week if they get the chance. I'd often forget Shane was still in bed. Or he'd get up as I was leaving to pick up Ciara from school, plonk himself at the kitchen table and ask in all seriousness, 'Is there any breakfast?' Er, no, because I'm just about to make your tea!

My sons went through that 'You're here to serve us and we know everything because we rule' stage. A lot of the time their behaviour was really frustrating, and sometimes it was downright hilarious. I remember on many occasions they'd be ranting at me about something or giving me the benefit of their opinion on the state of the world and after they'd left the room I'd just burst out laughing. They felt so strongly about things and I'd just be thinking, 'Oh boy, you have no idea what life is going to throw at you.' It's important never to make them feel stupid, though. I remember falling in love when I was about thirteen and my mum said, 'Oh shut up, Coleen, you don't know what love is,' and I hated her at that moment because I was absolutely heartbroken and I thought she didn't care. So when Shane or Jake confided in me about anything at all – however silly – I took it seriously. Even if I had a chuckle to myself later.

It's easy for parents to forget what a hard stage in life the teenage years are. Teens are plagued by insecurities, they break out in spots (both my boys got a bit of acne) and they keep getting told to 'grow up' but that they're 'too young' to do lots of other things. They're kind of in limbo, waiting to make the leap into adulthood.

People talk a lot about being there for your kids when they're little, but I think it's vital to be there for them when they're teenagers. When your kids are young, you know where they are at all times and you'd never leave them with anyone you didn't trust. And all they're worried about is whether they can play out in the rain or watch telly. Teens, on the other hand, are dealing with a big pile of new emotions and issues and they need you there, even if they don't show it.

They become very insular and as a mum you're always trying work out if they're telling you the whole truth. Shane or Jake would say to me, 'I'm just going round to my mate's to watch a film,' and I'd think, 'But are you, though? Hmmm, I'm not sure . . . ' There were probably twenty-five other teenagers doing it with them – it's called a party! Let's be honest, they start to get up to all sorts of things to see how far they can push the boundaries and, if you're not there to see it, that's when things can go wrong. I'm not saying it's easy, though. They won't let you get close to them – in fact a lot of the time it feels like they're trying to push you away, but that's all part of them growing up and trying to spread their wings.

I'm afraid you just have to grit your teeth and get through that stage of them being totally embarrassed to be seen with you and having to drop them off down a side street instead of outside the school gates. I'm happy to say that phase really doesn't last long and soon enough they'll be walking down the street with their arm round you and giving you big hugs in front of their friends. Well, that's what happened with me and my boys.

# He's Embarrassed by His Puppy Fat

**I like going swimming with my thirteen-year-old son but recently when I've suggested it he's refused, saying he's too fat. He only has a bit of puppy fat, but he's told me he's being bullied at school. How can I boost his self-esteem?**

When my son Jake was the same age he went through a body-conscious stage, too. He was always talking about getting more muscle in his legs. The fact is, kids of this age become very aware of their bodies and how they're developing. It's a huge thing for them so you have to treat it sensitively.

Tell your son if he's really unhappy about it, the best way to tone up every muscle is to go swimming regularly. Tell him you'll go with him as many times as he wants. And remind him there will be people of all shapes and sizes at the pool – and many will be bigger than him. Explain that most people feel a bit self-conscious in their swimsuits. You could say something like, 'I worry about people looking at my body, too, but we can go there together and show everyone how fit we are.' Also remind him that once he's in the pool no one can see him and no one cares. Hopefully, the more he goes, the more comfortable he'll become.

What you mustn't do is suggest he goes on a diet. Instead, encourage him by talking about all the benefits of being fit and healthy. Do things with him to help him lose weight without making a big deal about it – arrange family bike rides in the park, go on a nature trail, buy a badminton set for the garden. If it's fun, he's more likely to want to do it.

If he digs his heels in about the swimming, find another sport he enjoys that doesn't involve him getting half naked. Once he builds up his confidence I'm sure he'll go back to the pool.

One more thing: you must address the bullying straight away as this must be battering his self-esteem. Gently coax out of him what's been going on and speak to the school as soon as you can. This needs to be nipped in the bud. For more on this, see Beating the Bullies on page 215.

## Giving Them a Positive Body Image

Helping your teen develop a healthy body image is a real challenge for mums at the moment. With girls in particular there's an unhealthy obsession with weight and all their role models seem to be these teeny-tiny skinny celebrities with pinched faces and jutting collarbones. In my book, not attractive! I'm hoping that will change and by the time Ciara's a teenager we'll start seeing curvier, healthier (more realistic) young women for kids to aspire to on the covers of glossy magazines and on TV. In the meantime, I'm going to try my best to bring Ciara up to value more than just looks and to love her body – faults and all.

Here are my ways to help build your teen's body confidence:

- **Be a good role model.** Although my weight has gone up and down like a yo-yo and I've been on many diets in my time, I've always been very careful not to pass on my body hang-ups to Ciara. In fact, I never mention the dreaded D-word around her. When I've tried to lose weight in the past, I've always told her, 'I'm trying to get fit,' rather than, 'I'm on a diet,' so she sees it as a positive thing and associates it with being healthy.
- **Have a relaxed attitude to food at home.** Make meal times fun and sociable – don't ban foods; everything is fine in moderation – and eat healthily yourself so they follow your example.
- **Never tease them about their body.** Even if you're being jokey, teens are really sensitive and they'll take it to heart.
- **Focus on the inside.** Make sure you value their skills and attributes so they know these things are more important than what they look like. Praise them for being good at football or art, or for being funny and a great friend. This will really help to boost their self-confidence.
- **Explain that models get extra help!** Try to help them see

that the models and celebrities they want to look like have great lighting and make-up – not to mention a little help from the airbrush – to look that perfect in magazines. Trust me, I've been on many photoshoots in my time and I know what magic can be worked!

## Be alert to eating disorders!

Teens are the prime years for eating disorders like anorexia or bulimia to set in, and although they mostly affect girls, boys can suffer, too. Here's what to look out for . . .

- **Anorexia:** teens suffering from this will have a deep fear of being fat. As well as dramatic weight loss (or a failure to gain weight as they grow), watch out for them skipping meals, playing with their food instead of eating it, hiding food, lying about what they've had to eat, avoiding events where there will be food and being obsessed with weight and body image.
- **Bulimia:** youngsters with bulimia will eat huge amounts in one go then make themselves sick. They might be slightly overweight because of bingeing or their weight might fluctuate. They'll often disappear to the loo after a meal to

throw up what they've just eaten. Look out for food disappearing or being hoarded in their bedroom, they might get sore throats or have bad teeth because of vomiting, and they will be very concerned with weight and body image.

If you're worried about your teen, your first port of call should be your GP. You can also visit the Eating Disorders Association website www.b-eat.co.uk, which also has a youthline (0845 634 7650).

## I Worry For Her Safety Online

**My thirteen-year-old daughter has posted pictures of herself in a mini-skirt on a social networking site. She says it's harmless fun and all her friends put up similar pictures, but I'm worried she's sending out the wrong message and will get approached by dodgy men. What shall I say to her?**

Simple – tell her to unplug it! When my kids were in their early teens I'd only let them use the computer for homework. At first I felt bad because all their mates were using sites like these, but I stuck to my guns and I'm glad I did. I think thirteen is too young to be using these sites. And the fact that your daughter doesn't think there's anything wrong with posting these pictures on the net means she doesn't realize the risks – and that's a worry. If I were you I'd stop her using the site altogether. She will scream and holler and you'll be called the worst mum on the planet, but she'll get over it.

Failing that, explain to her that it won't just be kids her own age who have access to those pictures. Social networking sites do have privacy settings so you can control who sees her page online – get her to set it so only her friends can view her photos and information. In future, edit the photos she wants to post online and monitor the amount of time she spends on the computer, which should be in a family room where you can keep an eye on her. You can also buy software that filters out any sites you don't want her to have access to.

But be firm. You're the mum, after all and you're only trying to protect her.

# Should I Let Her Wear a Bikini on Holiday?

**We're about to go on a family holiday and my thirteen-year-old daughter wants to wear a little bikini on the beach. I'm worried about her sending out the wrong signals at such a young age – do you think I'm being crazy?**

It's hard nowadays because we're so frightened of everything and everyone, and it's tempting to want to wrap our kids up in cotton wool. But I do think it's a shame to have to worry about things like this. What's life come to if you go on holiday and have to worry about paedophiles lurking around every sand dune? But I don't think you're crazy – you've probably noticed your daughter's body is starting to develop and you just want to protect her. There's absolutely nothing wrong with your daughter wearing a bikini – as long as it's not an overtly sexy style with a tiny top and a thong. Get her one that's suitable for her age and maybe buy her some cute beach cover-ups such as a sarong to tie round her waist and a little sun dress. That'll make her feel really stylish and grown-up. When you get there you'll find there will be lots of other girls of the same age wearing bikinis and she might feel a bit dorky if she's not wearing one.

Just keep an eye on her as you would normally. Your holiday will be a great chance for her to make friends – and you don't want her to be left out if she doesn't fit in.

♥

## My Lazy Teen Won't Get Out of Bed!

**My fourteen-year-old son is on holiday from school, but he spends all day in bed. He sleeps until 1 p.m., then stumbles around in his pyjamas for most of the afternoon or plays on his computer. I want to get him out and enjoy the summer – go to the park or go swimming – but he won't listen to me. How can I get him to make the most of his school holidays?**

The thing kids love about summer holidays is that they don't need to get up early for school, so to expect your son to do that I think is too much. I know 1 p.m. sounds excessive – but didn't we all do this as kids? The great thing about summer is that it stays light for longer, so even if he does get up late he can still enjoy the day. Rather than kicking him out and saying, 'Go and do something!' why not plan some days out together – even if it's just once a week. He'll probably kick up a fuss to start with and say, 'Oh no, not with Mum!' but when Jake was your son's age I know he secretly loved a day out with me. Most teenagers don't like traipsing around a museum, so instead plan a trip to the beach or to a cricket match. Even if it's just a drive you'll still get him out of the house.

My other advice is to ration the amount of time he's allowed to spend on a computer to an hour a day. He'll probably tell you he hates you but that's what it is to be the parent of a teenager! And if he won't listen to the rules, just turn it off. That way he'll have fewer options – he'll have to get out and find things to do. For more on this, see My Summer Holiday Survival Guide on page 159.

## My Three Ways To . . .
## Deal With Teenage Mood Swings

**Don't overreact!** Remember, teens and moodiness go hand in hand. Their hormones are raging, they're coping with lots of new pressures – everything from exam stress to how they look – and the obvious person to take it all out on is, yup, you guessed it – *you*! When Shane or Jake were doing their best to wind me up, I'd leave the room, even if I was furious with them, then come back later and talk to them calmly. I often found that if I didn't take the bait and just let them blow off a bit of steam, they soon calmed down and I could talk to them sensibly.

**Find out if something's worrying them.** While mood swings are normal, if your teen is becoming withdrawn or aggressive there could be something more serious at the root of it. Maybe there's a problem at school or with one of their friends. Don't try to force it out of them, but remind them they can tell you anything at all – however serious they think it is – and you'll be there for them.

**Ask them to have some control.** Remind them that part of growing up is learning to control your emotions and think about how your moods affect other people. Ask them to consider what impact their moodiness is having on the rest of the family and point out that everyone is entitled to have a nice atmosphere at home.

## My Teenage Daughter Is Very Withdrawn

**My fifteen-year-old daughter seems very withdrawn and I don't know why. I've tried asking her but she won't open up to me. I know she keeps a diary and I'm tempted to read it. What should I do?**

The first thing I'd say is don't read her diary, because if she finds out she won't trust you again. Although if you think she's keeping something serious from you it'll be hard not to. Keep talking to her. Say, 'You know you can tell me whatever you want and we can deal with it together because that's what mums and daughters do.'

At fifteen her hormones will be out of control. Any number of things could be causing her to be withdrawn and as parents we jump to conclusions, but it could be as simple as being upset about a boy she likes or worrying about exams.

If she does open up to you, make sure you're prepared for what she tells you. And don't overreact because then she won't tell you anything again. I would also call her teacher to find out how your daughter has been behaving at school – have they noticed anything?

Why not plan a special day out for just the two of you so you can bond. It might help her to come out of herself a little and maybe she'll feel relaxed enough to open up to you.

## He's Heartbroken After Being Dumped

**My sixteen-year-old son was recently dumped by his girlfriend. They'd been together for six months and the split has left him heartbroken. His self-esteem has been knocked sideways and he just sits in his bedroom all the time feeling sorry for himself. I keep trying to explain it's not the end of the world, but he won't listen. How can I help him?**

Stop saying, 'It's not the end of the world,' for a start, because to him it is. When I was sixteen I broke up with a boyfriend and I remember that feeling so well. I also vividly recall my mum telling me that 'there are plenty more fish in the sea'. I wanted to kill her!

Talk to him as an adult. Even though he's sixteen and you know this will be the first of many break-ups, for him it's tough. Try saying, 'I know exactly how you feel, and I can tell you that with time you will get over it, so try to help yourself.' Why don't you plan an evening out and take him to do something he enjoys, such as a trip to the cinema with pizza afterwards? Encourage him to see his friends. If he says he doesn't feel like it, why don't you call his friends yourself and get them to come round? But do it sneakily so it doesn't look planned. The important thing is to make sure he knows you're taking it seriously and that you're there to support him. He may be only sixteen, but it's very real to him and a broken heart is a broken heart, whatever age you are.

# Should We Leave Our Son at Home Alone?

**My husband won't let my sixteen-year-old son stay in the house on his own when we go away for a weekend. I think he's mature enough but my husband doesn't. What would you do?**

I had this situation with Ray and my son Shane. We were going away and Shane wanted to be left alone, but Ray wanted him to come with the family. I thought he should be given the chance, but, as it turned out, Ray was right – Shane let us down. We came back to empty beer cans and realized he'd had his mates round. At sixteen, it's just too tempting to throw a party! And even if your child is behaving, others might not. My suggestion is that you gradually allow your son to earn your trust. Maybe leave him for a few hours, then slowly you can progress – although I'd wait a while before giving it a whole weekend. When you do decide to go ahead, tell him you are trusting him so he has to show you he's up to it.

A long time after Shane messed up, I told him I'd give him a second chance and if he blew that there would be no third chance. He didn't let us down that time and gradually renewed our trust. I'm sure with time your son will prove to be responsible, too.

## His Room Is a Tip!

**My sixteen-year-old son keeps leaving his room in a tip. It's causing so many arguments but nothing I say makes a difference.**

I went through the same thing with Shane Junior when he was a teen. We had lots of screaming matches about it, but I finally found a way to deal with it. I sat him down and said, 'You're now at an age where you want to be treated as an adult, but to be treated like one you have to act like one.'

I did one last big clean of his room from top to bottom, then I explained that from then on his bedroom was his domain. I told him that when his friends came over I'd make it clear to them the reason his room was such a mess was because I wasn't tidying it any more and shame him into feeling embarrassed about his space. He started bringing his washing down and collecting all the empty glasses in his room. Each time he did it, I acknowledged it and told him it was a big help to me. I didn't expect him to turn into Kim or Aggie overnight but I think he realized quite quickly how easy it is just to throw the covers over the bed and bring his rubbish down.

# She Keeps Saying She Hates Me

**My daughter is about to turn fourteen. Until last year she was a model student, but now she keeps getting low marks for her homework and has lost her focus. Her friend got an eyebrow pierced and she's determined to get hers done. We've argued every day since the topic was brought up. She keeps saying she hates me, and I don't understand. How can I get out of this mess?**

Your daughter has got to an age where she wants to stamp her personality on the world. It's hard for you to take a step back as a parent, but fighting with her will just make her want to rebel more. I don't like eyebrow piercings either but if her friends are having them I can see why she wants one. My advice would be to put the responsibility back on your daughter's shoulders. Cut a deal with her and say that when you see an improvement in her grades then you'll discuss the piercing. That way you're compromising with her and giving her time to really think about the piercing. You never know, by the time she's improved her grades she may have gone off the idea.

I always tell my kids they should be leaders rather than followers. If my son Jake comes home and says, 'So and so has this and I want it,' I say, 'Why don't you be your own person?' It does sink in eventually.

It's all about giving your daughter the confidence to be herself – and to understand she doesn't need to get her eyebrow pierced to fit in. But this will come with time.

And don't worry, your daughter does love you, even though it might not feel like it right now.

## She Has Too Many Male Friends

**My fourteen-year-old daughter has started hanging around with a group of boys. I've met them all and they're perfectly nice, but do you think it's a bit odd that she doesn't have any close female friends?**

No, I don't think it's odd at all. I was the same when I was a teenager. I got on better with boys and I felt less self-conscious around them. Girls can be bitchy, especially at that age, and I wasn't into all that competition about who had the best top or hairstyle. In fact, my best friend when I was growing up was a boy who lived next door. I got on with girls, too, but I preferred having a laugh with the boys rather than getting involved with all the gossiping the girls did. It was also nice to be the only girl, and therefore the centre of attention.

As long as your daughter is close to you and knows she can talk to you about female issues, I don't think you have any concerns. Just give her a sensible curfew and make sure you always know where she is. But if the boys are nice, like you say they are, and she's not giving you any other reasons to be concerned about why she's friends with them, then I don't think you need to worry. Having male friends may even be good for her – think of all the preparation she's getting for when she has to deal with men later in life!

## She's Going Out With an Older Boy

**My daughter, who is fourteen, has started going out with a sixteen-year-old lad. She's dyed her hair black, wears black make-up and has become moody and withdrawn. She's talking about getting piercings. I'm worried the next step will be alcohol and drugs. What can I do?**

You need to start asserting your authority now. At fourteen your daughter is still a child, lives in your house and should stick to your rules. You need to toughen up. Perhaps she is doing all this to find out where the boundaries are, because there don't seem to be any. Sometimes kids push and push because they want you to show some parental responsibility. It's a difficult age and she's rebelling.

With the clothes and the make-up she's obviously testing out the Goth look. Tell her, 'I'm letting you wear those clothes because you like them,' but if you don't want her to have piercings just say no. If she does get them done, punish her. Your daughter needs to know where to draw the line.

As for the older boyfriend, if you are OK with her seeing him there have to be firm rules. If you haven't already explained the consequences of underage sex to your daughter, do it now. There should be a strict curfew and you should always know where she is. If he's a nice boy he should respect that.

Just remember: you're the adult and what you say goes.

## Should We Trust the Boy She Met on the Net?

**My seventeen-year-old daughter has befriended a German boy, who's the same age, on a social networking site. I've seen his photos and he looks nice enough. She's planning to visit him but I'm really worried about it. What can I do to stop her going?**

Well, saying 'No' is always a good start. I'd be worried about this one, too. It's true, this person is probably a perfectly nice seventeen-year-old but, at the risk of sounding paranoid, he could also be an older man pretending to be a teenager. Let's face it, he could have posted anyone's photos on that site. Explain your worries to your daughter – she's old enough to understand why you're worried and to take it on board. Although she's a young adult at seventeen, she also lives at home, so therefore she must follow your rules.

If she's hell-bent on getting together with this boy, suggest he comes over here instead, so you can meet him. Maybe you could also get a phone number for his parents and speak to them. I also think at her age she's far too young to be travelling to another country on her own to meet someone she doesn't know – even if he is the same age.

Your daughter will probably hate you for interfering, but sit her down and explain to her that you're saying no because you love her and could never forgive yourself if something happened to her. If she really wants to meet this boy, she'll agree to him coming over here. Just make sure you're there when they meet. Sometimes as a mum you have to put your foot down, but you know you're doing the right thing.

# I Worry Her Clothes Are Too Sexy

**My fourteen-year-old daughter has taken to wearing mini-skirts and tight tops. She tells me they're fashionable, but I'm worried she's dressing too old for her age. How can I get her to see that her clothes are inappropriate for her age?**

I remember my niece doing something very similar when she was fourteen. It's very difficult because your daughter's a teenager and wants to fit in. When you look at other kids on the street, it's clear it is fashionable for teens to wear these clothes.

If I were you, I'd talk to her to see if you can come to a compromise. Explain that it's so much more attractive to leave something to the imagination rather than putting everything on display. Why don't you go shopping with her and pick out an outfit together? Be realistic, though – you're not going to get her to wear a skirt down to her ankles, but perhaps you can agree on a skirt that's a mini rather than a micro-mini. It may help if she brings one of her friends along, too, as she may be more likely to agree to an outfit if her friend likes it.

If the softly, softly approach doesn't work and she still digs her heels in, then go ahead and tell her, 'I'm not your friend, I'm your mum, and I won't let you go out like that.' Then check her bag before she leaves the house to make sure she hasn't hidden a change of clothes in there!

# I Think She's in With the Wrong Crowd

**My fourteen-year-old daughter has fallen in with the wrong crowd. I've overheard her friends swearing and talking about sex and alcohol. She has also started asking me to let her stay out later. Should I just ignore this or tell her what I think of her friends?**

This is tricky. The problem is, if you criticize her friends, it will just make her want to see them more. She'll also take it as a criticism of her judgement. But at the same time you shouldn't just ignore it if you feel these kids are a bad influence. I think you should tell her you'd like to get to know these friends better because you're a little worried she's hanging out with people you don't know very well. Ask her to invite them over to your house – maybe you'll see what she likes about them or you'll spot potential troublemakers.

As far as swearing and talking about sex is concerned, I wouldn't worry too much – it's a stage they all go through. But in terms of staying out, have a strict curfew and stick to it – explain the rules are there for her safety and because you love her. Build her confidence and say, 'Don't be a follower, be a leader.' Explain that she can say no to things and, if she does, you can guarantee there will be six friends like her who won't want to do it either. It just takes one person with the courage to say no. I always worried about Jake being influenced by friends. With certain issues I'd just say, 'You don't look cool if you do that. In fact, it makes you look younger.'

If you come down too hard, you'll have a battle on your hands. Keep talking to her and try to find a balance between being her parent and her friend. It's hard but it is possible.

## Knowing How Much Freedom to Give Them

Teenagers need to spread their wings, but they also need to know where the boundaries are. I gave Shane Junior and Jake a little bit more freedom in their mid-teens, but they were still on quite a tight rein and had to be in at a certain time every night. They were never allowed to hang around street corners till ten or eleven. But then they didn't want to either, because I had an open house policy. They were allowed to invite their mates over to sit in our kitchen and chat. It wasn't like everyone had to mind their manners – I left them alone so they felt comfortable being at our house. If they went to a friend's house, they'd still have to be home at 10 p.m. and in the winter it'd be earlier because it would be dark outside. I figured they wouldn't want to be out later unless they were up to no good! Of course they'd still whinge occasionally – 'But my friends can stay out till midnight!' – and I'd just reply, 'I don't care, they're not my children. If anything happened to you my life wouldn't be worth living.'

Surprisingly, teens actually quite like boundaries because it shows you care about them and it gives them a sense of security. I'd say to Shane and Jake, 'I'm trusting you by letting you out.' They hated feeling they'd let me down, so most of the time they were pretty good. But they also knew there would be consequences if they didn't stick to the curfew.

I also made sure I knew exactly where they were going, who they were with, what they were doing and how they were getting home. I always told my boys I'd pick them up from wherever they wanted me to, so they always felt they could call if they were in trouble.

♥

## How Can I Get Him to Revise?

**My sixteen-year-old is about to take his GCSEs but I'm convinced he hasn't done enough work for them. Whenever I go up to his room he has music on or is on the phone to a friend.**

**If I try to speak to him he just ignores me or tells me I don't understand. How can I get him to revise before it's too late?**

I went through the same thing with Shane Junior. His school told us he should be doing three hours' revision a night, but he was doing nothing. In the end we said, 'We can have screaming matches every day or we can meet halfway.' So we agreed that he had to do an hour's revision, then the rest of the night was his. It worked. Shane got into a routine and started doing his revision without us even nagging him.

Another tip is to give your son an incentive. It doesn't have to be as controversial as the trip to Amsterdam that I offered Shane (ahem, more of this later – see Sex, Drugs and Rock 'n' Roll on page 285), but you could promise cash. We told Shane we'd give him so much for an A grade and so much for a B or C. It was amazing – he did actually knuckle down.

On top of this, explain to him that this is the start of his adult life. I warned Shane Junior if he didn't pass any exams, then the day he got his results he'd have to go out and find a job – probably a naff one.

Amazingly, he did brilliantly and achieved ten GCSEs and got into college. And, in fact, he actually thanked us later because he knew he wouldn't have got them without our encouragement.

## My Three Ways To . . .
## Help Them Cope With Exam Stress

**Help them plan.** A lot of revision stress is the result of being disorganized and not knowing where to start. Help your teen come up with a realistic revision timetable to cover all the subjects they need to. They should feel calmer once they have something to work towards.

**Keep their energy levels up.** Make sure they're having regular meals and give them a supply of healthy snacks to keep them going. They should also take regular breaks or they won't be able to concentrate. Don't let them stay up too late revising before an exam. It's more beneficial to have a proper night's sleep than stay up too late cramming and being good for nothing the next day.

**Be positive.** They'll be nervous before an exam, some kids will even be terrified. So it's your job to reassure them that all they can do is their best and that's all you expect of them. Then give them a big hug and wish them good luck.

# *I Worry She Studies Too Much*

**I know this may sound odd but my fifteen-year-old daughter is spending too much time studying. I really think she needs to have a life, too. Where do you think I should start?**

I've only known parents who have arguments with their teenagers over them not working hard enough! But you're right to think she needs a life away from her schoolwork. If she's not interested in doing it herself, why don't you organize things for her? Say to her, 'Let's go out and go to the park or a gallery.' Maybe she doesn't want to just hang out with her friends because it doesn't interest her. Encourage your daughter and tell her you're really proud of her because you never have to tell her to study, but add that you think you should all go out more together. Ask her why she's studying so hard. Is she worried about failing? Is she stressed about her grades? Perhaps she just needs to be told she can only do her best and even if she does fail at something, you'll still be proud of her. Maybe that will help relieve the pressure a little. Also check how things are with her friends. Ask her what they do in their spare time – if she doesn't know, I think that's a bit of a worry. Explain that life is for having fun, too.

But remember, there are plenty of parents who would love to be in your boat because they can't get their kids to study for five minutes!

## My Three Ways To . . . Get Them Thinking About What They'll Do After School

**Make time to discuss it.** Sit down and talk to your teen when they start their final year at school. Find out their interests and what they fancy doing – do they want to go to college or find a job straight after school? Work experience is a good way of working out if a certain job is what they really want to do.

**Encourage them with schoolwork.** Be positive about them reaching their goals. That last year at school is tough with the pressure of exams looming and worries about finding a job or college place afterwards, so be as supportive as you can.

**Get them to consider alternatives.** Teenagers often change their minds or they may get turned down for a college course, so it's a good idea to get them thinking of other options.

# I Want Her to Study Closer to Home

**My daughter wants to go to university in Scotland. I think it's too far from our home in Bedford. We're so close, I'm not sure if I can cope with not seeing her every day. How can I make her change her mind?**

It's hard because you and your daughter have a close bond, but I think you should encourage her to go. It's a big world and she needs to experience life. She has a fantastic chance to get a great education. Think of the people who would love the opportunity to go to university but never get it.

If your daughter wants to go, and wants to try to stand on her own two feet, you have to back her. She'll need to know her mum is supportive, so try to be happy for her. It may seem a long way but it's not as though she'll be in Australia. If there are any problems, you can be there in a few hours.

My son Shane Junior went to work in Somerset and, while it was heartbreaking to wave him off and I missed him like mad, I was so proud, too. It's great when you see your kids becoming properly independent. I may not have seen him as often as I did, but there were always regular phone calls, texts and emails, so I was still very much part of his life.

When your daughter flies the nest, like all mothers waving their children off, you'll cry into your pillow at night, but you should also be really proud.

## My Three Ways To . . . Get Teens Ready For College

**Teach the basics.** If they don't know how to use the washing machine or the ironing board, now is the time to teach them. Talk them through the basics of how to keep things clean – better still, get them to practise at home first! You should also teach them a few easy recipes like macaroni cheese or spaghetti Bolognese.

**Safety first.** Invest in a carbon-monoxide monitor and a smoke alarm (teens are notorious for leaving candles burning, pots boiling and going out of the house without unplugging the iron or hair straighteners!). Remind them about staying safe when they're out drinking with their mates and the importance of making sure they don't walk home alone late at night.

**Get money wise.** If they don't already have a bank account, take them to open one. You should also sit down with them and plan a budget they can work to every month that includes everything from clothes to food and travel expenses. If you trust them, I would also set up a credit card for them – which you're responsible for paying for – in case of emergencies.

# He's So Lazy About Work

**My eighteen-year-old has just started a part-time job in a supermarket but he's lazy about work. He gets there late and I'm worried he'll get fired. How can I change his attitude?**

The truth is your son is now old enough to take responsibility for himself. It's not like school, when you could give them a sick note. He's an adult now.

Tell him that if he loses the job he won't be lying around in bed all day, and if he wants to go out at the weekend, you won't be giving him any money to spend. Kids reach the point where they want to be treated like adults but they don't act like one. When Shane Junior was seventeen and missed his bus to college, I refused to write him a note to explain what happened. I'd say to him, 'This is the first step of your life as a grown-up, how you act now will affect your future.' He also had to get a Saturday job to pay for the petrol and insurance on his car.

It's hard to stop being protective, but you have to take a step back – and let them make their own mistakes. Otherwise when he's twenty he'll still be thinking 'I can't be bothered.'

# They're Leaving Home . . . How to Cope With Empty Nest Syndrome

When my sons left home – Shane went off to be a Bluecoat at Pontin's and Jake went to theatre school – I actually missed the mess! It's funny because you spend so many years thinking, 'I can't wait for them to grow up and leave home.' But when they did go, I wanted to walk into their bedrooms and trash them . . . I suppose I just missed them, mess and all.

It made me panic a bit because it didn't seem that long ago I was rocking them to sleep when they were teething or holding their hands on that first day at school. I couldn't help thinking that in a heartbeat, it'd be Ciara's turn to leave. It made me realize how important it is not to completely give up your life for them, because they do leave and you're left thinking, 'What do I do now?'

It was hard at first when the boys left, but kids are like homing pigeons – they always return, usually when they want something and with two bin bags of washing! Here's how to make waving them goodbye a little easier . . .

- **Don't take it personally.** It's natural to feel upset and want them to stay, but you should feel proud that you've equipped them to stand on their own two feet. You've been a great mum!
- **Be excited for them.** Whether they're off to halls of residence at college or moving into their own place, take them shopping and help them pick out what they'll need for their new place. And be positive about their big step – they're probably feeling a bit scared and might need some encouragement.
- **Stay in touch.** Remember, they're only at the end of the phone. Shane and Jake are both pretty good at staying in touch with me – we all text a lot. Stay involved with your child's life and make it clear you're still there for them whenever they need you.
- **Home will always be home.** It sounds daft, but some kids might worry that now they've flown the nest, they shouldn't come back to stay. Tell them your house will always be their home and they're welcome any time. If they haven't moved too far away, invite them over for tea once a week to make the transition a little easier and catch up with each other.
- **Plan things together.** Organize weekends away, shopping trips or gatherings through the year when you can spend some proper time together as a family.
- **Finally, enjoy your free time!** Think of all that lovely time you'll have now you're not doing your teen's dirty laundry,

cooking their tea or chauffeuring them around from party to party. Rediscover all those things you love doing. Try evening classes, see your friends more and take holidays. It's also the perfect time to redecorate the house and get it exactly how you want it, now there's no inconsiderate teenager to mess it up!

TWELVE

# *Sex, Drugs and Rock 'n' Roll*

# Dealing With Risky Teenage Behaviour

I may as well start this chapter with the notorious Amsterdam scandal! Five years ago I became Public Enemy Number One when I said I'd pay for Shane Junior, a couple of mates and an adult to go to Amsterdam for a long weekend if he did well in his GCSEs. They asked me on *Loose Women* why I thought Shane wanted to go to Amsterdam and I said, 'I'm not an idiot, I know he's not going to smell the tulips!' Of course I knew he wanted to see the red-light district. I wasn't shocked. We have a very open relationship, so it wasn't as if I didn't know he was having sex. He was just acting his age and wanted to see the prostitutes in Amsterdam. When they asked on the show how I felt about that, I was just very truthful and said something along the lines of, 'To be honest, if he's going to try that, I would rather he went somewhere it was well policed and very clean than go to Magaluf for the weekend where the kids all get drunk and sleep with each other with no protection, so I haven't got a problem with it.'

Well, I can't tell you the uproar it caused – I was on the lunchtime news, in every paper and had radio stations calling up for interviews every five minutes. Suddenly it was, 'Coleen Nolan says she'll pay for her son to have sex!' I was criticized for having such a bad relationship with Shane that I was unable to talk to him about sex and would rather send him off to a prostitute! In fact, exactly the opposite was true. Shane and I were very close – we still are – and he'd already confided in me that he'd started having sex. I was simply trying not to be naive. Although all the publicity was awful at the time, I don't regret being outspoken now. I even got my 'Mum to Mum' column at the *Daily Mirror* as a result of those comments because they felt I had a refreshing attitude to parenting issues. The only downside of the whole thing was that Shane never got to go to Amsterdam!

## Talking to Them About . . . Sex

I think what the Amsterdam episode shows is that I do have a healthy, open relationship with my sons when it comes to discussing sex. Because sex was a taboo subject in my own family when I was growing up, I wanted my kids to feel comfortable talking to me about it. I wanted them to be prepared and to be safe. I started the sex talk quite early, not because I was condoning underage sex, but I didn't want to be naive and assume my boys wouldn't do it. So I said, 'I hope you're not having sex, because it's illegal and it can be disappointing as well as lovely.' But I also made sure they knew about contraception and the consequences of an unwanted pregnancy and sexually transmitted infections.

You have to judge with your own teen when the time is right. With my boys it was when I started to think their friendships with girls were more than just crushes. It's hard to acknowledge your baby's growing up and that they're even thinking about sex; you can choose to ignore it and pretend he's still into riding his bike, or you can accept the fact that he's riding it round to some girl's house. I'd rather know about it.

Shane was fifteen when we had the talk about when he might have sex. He was becoming obsessed with girls – every pop video he'd watch he'd say, 'Oh, she's fit!' So we sat down and discussed it. I told him he needed to understand the importance of using a condom and, at the end of the chat, I said I'd like to know when he did it. A few months later, he came into the kitchen where I was doing the washing-up and told me he'd lost his virginity. I had my back to him at the time and I wanted to slide down on to the floor and cry! But I kept my voice steady and before I could get the sentence out he said, 'Yes, I did.' He knew I was going to ask if he'd used a condom.

It's also important to teach them about boundaries when it comes to sex and that no means no, and that they should treat their partners with respect. Shane was going out with girls who were mad about him, then he'd dump them and turn up the next night with one of their mates. They'd be devastated. I told him he mustn't lead girls to think he wanted a relationship with them, then act like he didn't care. I told him he had to be honest from the start and to treat his girlfriends as he'd like to be treated himself. He behaved well after that.

Teens don't respond well to lectures, so I really believe the best way to talk to them about sex is to have an ongoing dialogue at home, so they feel comfortable bringing things up with you and will confide in you if they have any problems. It worked for me and my boys, and I'll be doing the same thing with Ciara when she's old enough.

# She Has Love Bites on Her Neck

**My thirteen-year-old daughter came back from a party with love bites on her neck. She tries to hide them from me by pulling her jumper up to her chin. I'm worried it'll lead on to her having sex. She's so young I can't bear to think about it. What should I do?**

Oh, dear. If our daughter came home with them, I would leave the country before her dad saw them – regardless of whether she was thirteen or thirty!

Be open with her. Tell her you know what she's got on her neck and try to find out what's going on and who she's been snogging. Hopefully, you've had a conversation about the facts of life already, but if you haven't, you should have it now. Also explain how ugly love bites are and that no one thinks they're cool. Try to stay calm, though. There's no point throwing a fit because that will just push her away.

At thirteen you do stupid things and it's probably just a case of her experimenting and thinking she's so grown-up because she has a love bite. I'm sure when you bring it up she'll be really embarrassed and, initially, she probably won't want to talk about it. But if you persevere and don't get angry, then you can chat sensibly about it. I'm sure you don't have too much to worry about, but keep a careful eye on her and who she's hanging out with.

# Could My Son Be Gay?

**I was using the internet the other night when I looked at the history of what had been looked at before and saw someone had been logging on to a gay dating website. The last person to use the computer was my seventeen-year-old son. Do you think I should say something?**

First things first – you don't know why he was looking at it. He might have been doing it out of interest or for a laugh. But if it's because he's gay, then it's a subject you need to tread carefully with. I wouldn't specifically tell him that you've seen what he's been looking at. If you do that you might back him into a corner and he might say, 'I was just looking at it for fun,' and you'll never know his true feelings.

How you act depends on your feelings about him possibly being gay. If you have a problem with it, then my advice would be to keep your opinions to yourself or he'll never open up to you. If you are comfortable with it, though, then make it clear that you are. Don't give specifics; instead drop things into conversation. Perhaps if something is on TV, make a joke and say, 'You know, if that was you I wouldn't mind.' Let him know you're OK with it. The majority of boys want to tell their mums they're gay, rather than their dads. So try to be there for him. At the end of the day if he's gay, he's gay and he'll tell you when he's ready. He'll still be the same person he was yesterday, he'll just need the love and support of his mum even more.

♥

## She Wants to Go on the Pill

**My fifteen-year-old daughter wants to go on the Pill. As far as I know she doesn't have a boyfriend and I can't see why she should have to take it. What should I do?**

Firstly, I think it's fantastic your daughter told you she wants to do that. But now you need to sit her down and ask why she feels she needs to be on the Pill. Some fifteen-year-olds take it for medical reasons (for example, to control heavy periods), but if it's because she wants to have sex, then now is your chance to talk to her about it. Not only should you make it clear that it's against the law at her age but also tell her you think she's still too young. Have a calm, grown-up conversation with her. You're obviously a good mum because your daughter feels she can discuss these things with you, so take advantage of that. Explain that if it's about peer pressure because all her friends say they are doing it, she shouldn't feel she needs to as well. Also explain to her that she'll be taking powerful hormones every day, which most women wouldn't want to do if they didn't have to. Say to her that the first time she has sex should be special and nobody will think badly of her if she doesn't feel ready for it yet. If they do, they're not worth knowing anyway.

If she tells you it's because she wants to have sex, then tell her she needs to think very seriously about it. She needs to know about other forms of contraception to prevent sexually transmitted diseases including chlamydia, genital warts and HIV.

All you can do is make sure she knows everything she needs to know about sex before having it and keep talking to her so she feels able to confide in you.

## What to Do When She Says She's Pregnant

This is what every mum of a teenage girl dreads happening, but it's crucial you stay calm. Remember, she probably didn't plan it and she's probably terrified of the situation she's found herself in – and she'll be worried about your reaction, too. Concentrate on reassuring her and trying to work out what she wants to do about the baby. She might not know how many weeks pregnant she is, so take her to see the GP to get checked out and discuss what her options are. Be prepared for the fact that you might not agree with her decision, but you have to try to put your personal feelings aside and support her.

I got pregnant accidentally when I was only sixteen and I was terrified. I ended up telling nobody apart from my boyfriend and we went to a clinic in Harley Street together so I could have an abortion. It was heartbreaking. I wish I'd felt able to confide in someone, but my parents didn't know I was seeing anyone, let alone having sex. I felt incredibly ashamed and I didn't want to hurt them.

So when Shane Junior had a scare a few years ago I made sure I was there for him. He told me his girlfriend's period was late, so I asked if she'd bought a pregnancy test and he said no. I suggested he bring her to the house and I told her I'd buy the test. She was frightened of telling her mum, but I reassured her that if it did turn out she was pregnant we'd go to see her mother together. It was exactly the kind of support I'd needed when I was sixteen.

It turned out that Shane's girlfriend wasn't pregnant, but the incident made me realize that times haven't changed that much. We all think our kids are so streetwise these days, but they're just kids and they panic. They're still frightened you'll react badly and don't want to let you down.

It's hard not to go bananas when you're faced with a situation like this because it means your child has had unprotected sex, and you've always told them not to. But you have to stay calm, otherwise they'll never come to you with a problem again. You can still let them know you're not happy – I made sure Shane knew I was disappointed in him. As a mum of two boys I'd always been very clear that if they did get a girl pregnant, they would never walk away from the situation as long as I was alive. If there was a baby, they'd be part of its life. I think it's vital to teach boys that sense of responsibility because, at the end of the day, they do get off lightly.

# I Found Porn in His Room

**I found porn in my fifteen-year-old son's bedroom. Should I ignore it or should I say something?**

He sounds like a pretty typical fifteen-year-old boy! In my opinion you should ignore it. Both my sons have gone through that stage and I really don't think it's a problem. You do get people who think it's disgusting, but usually boys are just discovering women's bodies and what everything is for. I don't think it's something you need to get concerned by or talk to him about.

I actually think he'd be mortified if you did make a big thing of it. I know you probably don't want to think about it, but masturbation is a normal, healthy part of growing up and how you react to it could affect his future sexual relationships. If you make him feel ashamed, it could scar him for life. You really mustn't make him feel like it's wrong and unhealthy. It would be hard to find a teenage boy in this country who hadn't looked at porn. When my son bought a girly mag he told me. I didn't act embarrassed or shocked because I knew if I did he wouldn't confide in me again.

Obviously, if you'd found hardcore porn you might be right to worry – and then you should bring it up with him. But if it's normal, then leave it. I can assure you he's no different from any other straight boy his age.

# Should I Let Them Share a Bed?

**My sixteen-year-old son has been dating his girlfriend for a couple of months now and I'm pretty sure they're sleeping together. He's asked if she can come and stay on Saturday night. I'm not sure if I feel comfortable with them sharing a bed. What shall I do?**

I wouldn't feel comfortable with it either. If they've only been together a couple of months, then I think it's too soon. I told Shane Junior that if he'd been with someone for six months and it was still going strong, and looked like it was turning into a serious relationship, then maybe I'll let her come to stay. He never complained about that. It's not good for siblings to see their elder brother bringing home different girls all the time. If I were you, I'd tell your son, 'If you're still going out with her in another three or four months then we'll talk again. But I have to see that it's a serious relationship before I let you have girlfriends to stay over.'

I know it won't stop him having sex, but it's all about respect – for their partner and for you. And make sure you emphasize the importance of safe sex. I've actually bought condoms for my son. I just think that if you know they're doing it, don't turn a blind eye. I don't want to be a grandma just yet!

## Talking to Them About . . . Alcohol

When Shane was fourteen, I got a call from one of his friends asking if I'd come round to pick him up because he had stomachache. It was about ten o'clock at night and as soon as I put the phone down I thought, 'He's drunk.' When I picked him up he was absolutely slaughtered. The kids had been left in the house on their own and they'd raided the drinks cabinet; Shane had drunk a bottle of vodka virtually by himself. It was then I realized that sometimes it doesn't matter how much you talk to them, they're going to do their own thing.

What I was pleased about was that Shane still felt he could call me, even though he knew he'd messed up badly. He threw up for twenty-four hours. To this day I don't know how he didn't end up in hospital, but it put him off ever doing it again.

I didn't go bananas at Shane when I was driving him home because there was no point. I remember him saying, 'Mum, I know you're going to lecture me over this, but can you do it in the morning?' The next morning we grounded him for three weeks and I explained to him calmly the seriousness of what he'd done. I said, 'It could so easily have been the hospital that had called me last night, telling me you'd died from alcohol poisoning.' He took it all in and didn't complain.

When I realized Shane was obviously interested in drinking I tried to control it. So when he was sixteen and we were having a family party at the house, rather than banning him from having anything to drink, which would probably only make him want to get his hands on alcohol even more, I'd say he could have two drinks. He was allowed one at the start of the evening and one at the end of the night.

All you can do is warn them of the dangers of drinking too much and hope that whatever happens and however much trouble they think they're in, they know to call you.

## My Three Ways To . . . Discuss Sensible Drinking With Your Teen

**Explain the consequences.** Help them to see that drinking too much seriously affects their judgement and they may do something they regret later. Teenagers don't realize the dangers; they just think drinking is a big laugh. It's important you explain they could put their life at risk if they're falling-down drunk.

**Tell them what's acceptable.** Discuss with them what amount of drinking you feel is acceptable at their age. Remind them that it's illegal to buy alcohol before they're eighteen.

**Make sure they know *how* to drink.** If you accept they're going to drink, make sure they know how to drink, for example that spirits are served in small measures and are usually mixed with something else. Show them what a full measure of spirits looks like so they know not to drink half a pint of neat gin or vodka. And warn them off accepting drinks when they don't know what's been put into it, like punch at a party.

# I Saw My Thirteen-Year-Old Drinking

**Last weekend I drove past the local off-licence and saw my thirteen-year-old swigging from a bottle of cider with some friends. I want to confront him about it, but I don't know how to do it without pushing him into a corner and making him more secretive about things in the future.**

My approach would be to say calmly that you saw him drinking, explain why this worries you and talk about the effect alcohol has on the body. You could also get some information together so he can read about the side effects. Don't lecture him, though. I always get the best out of my boys when I talk to them as adults. Find out if he's trying to impress anyone. It's so easy at that age to feel pressured into doing things because your friends are doing them. Address the issue of who he's hanging out with – are they older boys?

You should also impress on him that it's against the law, and get him to think about the repercussions if he's caught drinking in the street by the police.

He's incredibly young to be drinking, so you need to keep a close eye on this. Perhaps you shouldn't allow him to hang round street corners with these boys. Give him a strict curfew and stress there will be consequences if he doesn't stick to it. If

I were you, I'd ground him for a few days so he realizes the seriousness of what he's done. He needs to appreciate he can't do it again.

## I Think My Son's Smoking

**I found a packet of cigarettes in my fourteen-year-old son's room while I was cleaning it last week. I don't know what to do. I don't want him to think I was snooping, but then I'm so angry and don't want him to be smoking at such a young age.**

I've been here before with my own son. I think it's important you address this issue immediately. Don't feel you're snooping in his room – the truth is you were tidying it so I wouldn't feel worried about that.

Perhaps one way to approach it would be to sit him down and say, 'A neighbour spotted you smoking and I think we should have a chat about it.' That way you don't need to admit you found his cigarettes in his bedroom. The next step is to talk to him about the dangers of smoking – everything from how it might affect his fertility in the future to heart problems and lung cancer. You should also say that while he might think it's cool, no girl likes to kiss a boy with cigarette breath and nicotine-stained teeth!

The problem I had with my boys is that I'm a smoker myself, so in order not to sound like a hypocrite, I explained how I wished I wasn't addicted to cigarettes myself and how awful it is to be a smoker.

If you find your son is still smoking after your chat then lay down rules and tell him he will be grounded if he continues to smoke.

## Talking to Them About . . . Drugs

I've always had major talks to Shane and Jake about drugs and I probably put the fear of God into them! I stressed that for things to go terribly wrong it could take only one time and one bad drug. They could be that one person in a million to end up in a coma – and they may have taken a drug only once.

The trouble is, these days drugs are so easily available to kids. Some boys Shane and Jake know have been offered cocaine. Shane told me when he started going out properly at eighteen he was offered drugs everywhere he went. It's so different to when I was their age. I didn't know anything about drugs and I was in a band. I thought I was hip and cool if I had a fag.

It's such a worry for parents, but you have to get clued up on the issue. Here are a few pointers . . .

- **Know your facts.** The chances are your teens will know a lot more about drugs than you do, so before you tackle the subject with them, do some research into what drugs there are and what they can do to you. Arm yourself with some real facts and statistics so you know what you're talking about and your children will take you more seriously.
- **Give them confidence.** A lot of kids feel pressured into taking drugs by their mates because they don't want to look uncool. Explain to them that it's much more cool to be their own person and be strong enough to say no. If they're offered drugs, they may feel more confident turning them down by saying something like, 'No thanks, I'm just not into those,' so they get themselves out of the situation and save face, too.
- **Look out for warning signs.** If you suspect your child is taking drugs, look out for changes in behaviour such as mood swings, sleeping more, being secretive, locking themselves away for hours, changing their group of friends and losing interest in their appearance. For more information and advice you can call FRANK on 0800 77 66 00 or visit www.talktofrank.com. Visit www.addaction.org.uk for advice and support, and to find a local drug and alcohol treatment centre. Visit www.drugscope.org.uk for the latest

information about drugs and a directory of where to get help.

- **Remind them it's illegal.** Explain they could get a criminal record if they're found guilty of possessing or supplying drugs, which can affect everything from a university application and future job prospects to preventing them from being allowed entry to certain countries such as the USA. Here are the penalties for different drug types:
  - **Class A** (this includes cocaine, ecstasy, heroin, LSD and crystal meth). Possession can lead to a prison sentence of up to seven years and an unlimited fine. Supplying (including giving it to a friend) could lead to a life sentence and/or an unlimited fine.
  - **Class B** (this includes speed and cannabis). Possession could get you up to five years in jail as well as an unlimited fine. Supplying it can get you up to fourteen years in jail and/or an unlimited fine.
  - **Class C** (this includes ketamine and tranquillizers). It's illegal to possess tranquillizers without a prescription. Possession of drugs in this class can get you up to two years in prison and/or an unlimited fine. Supplying could mean fourteen years in jail and/or an unlimited fine.

## He Has a Sudden Interest in Drugs

**My fourteen-year-old has started asking me lots of in-depth questions about drugs and taking a sudden interest in them. Should I worry that he's tried something?**

I wouldn't panic and think he's become a drug addict, but don't ignore it either. Jake was thirteen when he came home and started talking about the differences between cocaine and heroin. In his case, as it most likely is with your son, they had just started learning about drugs at school.

Perhaps your son is too embarrassed to put his hand up in class and wants to know more about it from you? It could also be that his friends are talking about it, especially as drugs are in the news a lot. It's very likely he just has a natural interest in what's happening. Why don't you ask him? Just say, 'What's the sudden interest? Have your friends been talking about them?'

There's always the chance he's been offered drugs at school, so just ask him gently if that's the case. If he says no, it might still be worth having a word with his teacher to find out if they've had any problems with kids dealing drugs at school.

It's always best to answer your son's questions and talk about things openly, so he feels he can come to you with problems in the future and know that you'll react calmly. Gather as much information as possible so you can answer each question he asks fully. And remember not to leave out all the really bad things about drugs, so he is aware of the dangers.

THIRTEEN

# Every Mum's Christmas Problems Solved!

# How to Turn Your Little Devils into Christmas Angels

It's exhausting being a mum at Christmas: there's all that over-excitement, far too much chocolate, squabbles with siblings – and that's just you!

I'm a big kid at Christmas – I absolutely love it. When I was growing up, Christmas at our house was always magical and I wanted to recreate that for my children. There were eight of us kids so we each got just one present from Santa, but my God it was so special. That present was the thing you'd wanted all year and I can't tell you how exciting it was to come downstairs on Christmas morning and see it under the tree.

I have to admit that now I have children of my own I'm one of those mums who goes a bit over the top on presents. It's the one time of the year when I have an excuse to spoil the kids. The rest of the time I'm pretty strict and Shane, Jake and Ciara don't get everything they want handed to them on a plate, so at Christmas I go to town.

At our house every Christmas Eve is crazy because the kids are always too excited to go to sleep. Even though the boys are now seventeen and twenty-one I still won't put their presents out till they're in bed, so we're usually up till four or five in the morning. Ray's always building something and I'm frantically wrapping the gifts.

But, let's be honest, as well as all the fun and excitement, Christmas brings its own stresses and strains, so here are my tips on keeping things festive . . .

# How to . . . Explain to Family You Want to Be on Your Own For Baby's First Christmas

This is one lots of new mums are faced with. The grandparents are desperate to see their new grandchild, but all you want to do is stay at home and enjoy your first Christmas together as a family. I'm afraid there's no way round it: you just have to be honest. Most grandparents will understand this is a special time for you – all they have to do is think back to when you were a newborn and I bet they wanted to do exactly the same thing. If you live nearby, I'm sure they'd appreciate it if you popped in for an hour or so on Christmas morning to exchange gifts and so they can see the baby. You don't want to hurt anyone's feelings, so arrange another date during the holidays when you can spend the whole day with them.

# How to . . . Tell the Kids You Can't Afford to Splurge on Presents

You want to give your kids everything they desire so this is a tough one, but when it comes to young children you've got the perfect scapegoat – Santa. Explain he can't bring everything on their list because he's got to take presents to all the other boys and girls in the world. Ask them to pick one favourite thing. If their choice is still too costly, say, 'I don't think Santa can bring so many big expensive presents this year.' If you have older kids, just be honest. Tell them how much you have to spend on them, then they can have a proper think about what it is they really want. If you prepare them in advance, it'll avoid disappointment on Christmas morning.

It's really not worth going into debt to give them fabulous presents because, knowing kids, they'll be bored with them in two weeks, but you'll still be paying off your credit cards for months to come.

# Can I Stop My Girls Fighting Over Gifts?

**My two daughters, aged five and six, are very competitive. Every Christmas and birthday they fight over each other's presents. How can I make sure it doesn't happen this year?**

When my kids were younger, I noticed that at some point on Christmas Day my son Jake always wanted what Shane had, even if it wasn't on his list. So I began getting them the same things, or a variation of the same thing. Then there's nothing to be jealous of. Some people will say it's ridiculous and a waste of money to buy the same presents but, if it keeps the peace and all the kids are happy, I say why not? It's also worth reminding greedy children how lucky they've been to get the presents on their list and that Santa might not be quite so generous next year if he sees they've been naughty.

# How to . . . Deal With Over-Excitement

The problem with Christmas these days is that the build-up starts in October and kids just can't wait. As soon as the TV ads for toys start (which seems to be earlier each year), the pestering begins.

My way of dealing with any bad behaviour in the run-up to Christmas is to say, 'Don't forget Santa's watching and he'll cross things off your list if you're naughty.' That tends to do the trick. On Christmas Day itself the kids get up so early and there's always so much running around that by lunchtime they're exhausted. When Ciara was three or four, I'd get her to take one of her new toys up to bed so she could have a rest. Another idea is to space out the gifts – give them their main present in the morning, then a second after lunch and a third in the evening. That way the excitement doesn't end all at once, leaving the rest of the day as a letdown. We actually keep a present back for Ciara and give it to her on Boxing Day – that way she appreciates each gift more.

Remember, though, it's the one day of the year that kids should be allowed to go a bit nuts, so have a festive tipple and relax!

## How to . . . Stop Them Overindulging in Sweets and Chocolate

For kids, chocolate is simply nicer than turkey, so don't give them a selection box until they've had their Christmas roast. If they don't know you have it, they won't miss it. In my house the chocolate doesn't come out until the afternoon. I give Ciara her selection pack after dinner so it's another little gift to open. Also if you keep the sweets till after the meal they'll be full up so won't eat as many of them.

## How to . . . Explain Santa to Sceptical Kids

This is easy – just make sure you rent *The Santa Clause* movie starring Tim Allen. It explains it all in there: how he gets into flats and homes with no chimneys – everything. I watch it with

Ciara every Christmas Eve and by the time I go to bed even I believe in him!

It's sad, though, when they find out there's no Father Christmas. I was so upset when Jake was told by his teacher that Santa didn't exist – he was only six. I wanted to keep my kids believing for as long as possible. There does come a point when they start hearing things from friends, but my response would always be, 'Well it's never been proved there is a Father Christmas, but it's never been proved there isn't one, either.' See how long you can get away with it!

Even now I look out of the window on Christmas Eve and say, 'I'm looking for Santa.'

## How Can I Have a Happy Day Without My Daughter?

**I split up with my ex when our four-year-old was a baby. It's his turn to have her on Christmas Day and I'm dreading not having her around. I'll be with family and my new boyfriend but how will I get through it all?**

I don't know what kind of relationship you have with your ex, but maybe you could arrange to pop in for a couple of hours in the morning to give your daughter her presents. If not, why not turn Boxing Day into a very special second Christmas Day? You could keep some presents back to give her then. It will be hard for you not to be with her on the day itself, but it's fantastic that you're being so fair when it comes to sharing her.

After I'd separated from Shane and the boys were still little we always made sure he was there on Christmas morning. He'd get to our house about 6 a.m. and I'd wake up the boys so he could see them open their presents. I felt it was the right thing to do. Now the boys are grown-up and Shane's got two young children, they see each other between Christmas and New Year.

## How to . . . Cope With Stroppy Teens

Teenagers just love to be stroppy and anti-social at Christmas. Most would rather spend the day watching telly in their room or Facebooking their mates than sit down to Christmas dinner with the family. It's so uncool! My philosophy is, if they want to sulk in their bedroom let them do it. It's not fair on the rest of the family to spoil Christmas with arguments. Take a tray of food up to them if you have to. In my experience they'll get bored and join you eventually. Or you could try compromising.

For example, say: 'I'd like you to eat with us, so why don't you just give us two hours of your time, then you can spend the rest of the day in your room?'

You could also try involving them in things on the day – ask them to sort out the music or the entertainment for the evening, whether that's board games or karaoke. Sometimes teenagers feel a bit awkward and isolated from the rest of the family, so maybe you have to be the one to make an extra effort to get them involved in the preparations. You could also agree to them having a friend round in the evening or for them to go to a mate's house once dinner is over.

Another thing teens usually complain about is visiting an elderly relative over the Christmas holidays, but I think it's important to teach them to be caring and respectful. It's all part of growing up. I remember sitting my boys down and saying, 'That'll be me one day,' which helped them to understand.

Remember, it's a teenager's job to be tricky at Christmas, but they do grow out of it!

# *Help! My In-Laws Hate Our Noisy Children*

**Every Christmas ends in disaster for us as we go to my husband's parents' house. They're really old-fashioned and believe kids should sit quietly at the dinner table then play quietly with their toys. And my kids (they're seven and five) are just not like that. My husband gets anxious they're not behaving, then I get cross with him for taking his parents' side. What can I do?**

Um, don't go there for Christmas! Or, if you really have to go, stand up for yourself. It's Christmas Day, for God's sake. Say, 'I'm afraid I can't guarantee the kids will be quiet all day.' If that's going to be a problem for them, suggest they come to your house instead so if it's too much for them they can always leave. Otherwise, why not go to theirs for a couple of hours in the morning?

Maybe it's time you made the break and started spending the day at your own house and visit relatives on Boxing Day. For me Christmas is all about the children, so you should put them first. It's the one day of the year when they can get boisterous and not be told off!

It's a shame because it sounds like Christmas is a stressful event for you each year and causes tension between you and your husband. I think it's time you started putting your family first . . . and have some well overdue fun!

# Useful Contacts and Further Information

### *For Mums With Little Ones*

**www.babycentre.co.uk**: advice and information from pregnancy onwards.

**www.bliss.org.uk**: support for parents of premature and sick babies. Phone: 0500 618 140.

**www.mama.co.uk**: Meet-A-Mum Association – support and friendship for all new mums, particularly those feeling lonely and isolated after the birth.

**www.mumsnet.com** and **www.netmums.com**: share tips and experiences with other mums.

**www.ncma.org.uk**: the National Childminding Association can help you find a registered childminder in your area.

**www.nct.org.uk**: the National Childbirth Trust will have a local branch for support through pregnancy and early parenthood. Pregnancy and birth line: 0300 3300 772. Breast-feeding line: 0300 3300 771.

## *Health and Nutrition*

**www.eatwell.gov.uk**: the Food Standards Agency for healthy eating information.

**www.blossomcampaign.org**: information on childhood allergies.

**www.b-eat.co.uk**: Eating Disorders Association. Youthline: 0845 634 7650.

**www.asthma.org.uk**: a charity which offers advice on asthma. Phone: 0800 121 6244.

**www.firstaid.org.uk**: This Scotland-based organization offers first-aid training in the UK. Phone: 0141 332 4031.

**www.nhsdirect.nhs.uk**: A useful first point of call for minor health queries. For England and Wales, phone: 0845 4647; for Scotland, phone: 0845 424 2424.

## *Learning and Revision*

**www.early-education.org.uk**: British Association for Early Childhood Education. Phone: 020 7539 5400.

**www.bbc.co.uk/schools**: interactive learning and revision site for primary and secondary students.

**www.channel4learning.com**: education resources, games and activities for primary and secondary kids.

***Let's Talk About Sex* by Robie H. Harris**: book aimed at kids from nine years old.

**www.nagcbritain.org.uk**: advice for parents of gifted children. Phone: 0845 450 0295.

## *Family Support*

**www.fsid.org.uk**: the Foundation for the Study of Infant Deaths gives support for bereaved families and safe sleeping advice. Helpline: 0808 802 6868.

**www.oneparentfamilies.org.uk**: One Parent Families/ Gingerbread. Phone: 0800 018 5026.

**www.parentlineplus.org.uk**: parenting advice from babies to teens. 24-hour helpline: 0808 800 2222.

**www.childbereavement.org.uk**: offers support for when a child dies, or when a child is bereaved. Support line: 01494 446648.

**www.nfm.org.uk**: National Family Mediation for advice and support for divorcing or separating parents.

**www.talktofrank.com**: FRANK offers parents and young adults no nonsense advice on drugs. Helpline: 0800 77 6600.

**www.addaction.org.uk**: for help with addiction.

**www.drugscope.org.uk**: DrugScope gives support and advice on drugs and alcohol for adults and young people.

**www.beatbullying.org**: advice on bullying for young people and parents.

**www.bacp.co.uk**: British Association for Counselling and Psychotherapy to find a qualified therapist in your area.

**www.relate.org.uk**: relationship counselling. Phone: 0300 100 1234.

### *Support for Kids*

**www.childline.org.uk**: confidential support for kids. Phone: 0800 11 11.

**www.cybermentors.org.uk**: a site where young people can support each other against bullying online.

**www.rd4u.org.uk**: Cruse Bereavement Care site for young people. Helpline: 0808 808 1677.

# Acknowledgements

I'd like to thank my children, Shane Junior, Jake and Ciara, because without them this book wouldn't have been possible. They were also very generous in allowing me to include so many embarrassing stories about them! My husband Ray deserves a special mention for being a great dad and wonderfully supportive of everything I do. I'd also like to thank Claire Higney at the *Daily Mirror* for all her help with my book. And, of course, a huge thank-you to all the mums who've contributed to my parenting column over the years.

# Index

Page references in **Bold type** denote complete chapters

## J



## K



## L



## M



## N

## S

## T